PUT IT IN WRITING

PUT IT IN WRITING

New message

To

Subject

A Straightforward Guide to Preventing Workplace Misunderstandings and Costly Mistakes

Send

MEIRA SPIVAK

Copyright © 2026 by Meira Spivak.

All rights reserved.

No portion of this book may be reproduced in any form without written permission from the publisher or author, except as permitted by U.S. copyright law.

This publication is designed to provide accurate and authoritative information in regard to the subject matter covered. It is sold with the understanding that neither the author nor the publisher is engaged in rendering legal, investment, accounting or other professional services. While the publisher and author have used their best efforts in preparing this book, they make no representations or warranties with respect to the accuracy or completeness of the contents of this book and specifically disclaim any implied warranties of merchantability or fitness for a particular purpose. No warranty may be created or extended by sales representatives or written sales materials. The advice and strategies contained herein may not be suitable for your situation. You should consult with a professional when appropriate. Neither the publisher nor the author shall be liable for any loss of profit or any other commercial damages, including but not limited to special, incidental, consequential, personal, or other damages.

ISBN (paperback): 979-8-9933525-0-3
ISBN (hardcover): 979-8-9933525-1-0
ISBN (eBook): 979-8-9933525-2-7
ISBN (audiobook): 979-8-9933525-3-4

To my husband, who patiently put up with me while I wrote this book—even during our road trip. He is always by my side, with humor, wisdom and kindness. Thank you to my incredible children, parents, in-laws and extended family, who show constant support for all my projects.

Contents

Preface   11

   Who Is This Book For?   13

   How The Book Works   14

PART I

Chapter One
The Basics of Documentation   19

   Legal Protection   23

   Contracts   30

   Expense Reimbursement   41

   Policies   44

   Accountability and Driving Sales and Recruitment   56

   Project Management   63

   Accurate Finances   68

Chapter Two
Hiring & Firing   73

   Job Description   73

   Firing   81

   Working Conditions   84

Contracts	85
Terminating—and Beginning—Partnerships	87
Exit Interviews	89

Chapter Three
Documentation for Effective Leadership — 91

Policy Exceptions	91
Decision-Making for Life	92
Indecisiveness	96
Scheduling and Calendaring	96
Clarifying Thoughts and Feelings	98
Allowing Others to Help	102
Company Culture	103
Exit Planning and Succession	105

Chapter Four
What *NOT* to Put in Writing — 109

Guiding Principle #1: When it's something you might later regret writing	110
Guiding Principle #2: When it's something that can be taken out of context and shared	113
Guiding Principle #3: When it's something you don't want recorded for posterity	114
Guiding Principle #4: When it should really be a conversation and you were avoiding discomfort	115

PART II

Chapter Five
The Art of Setting Goals—Why Documentation Is a Necessity   123

- How to Choose a Goal   124
- S-M-A-R-T Goals   127
- How Our Efforts Are Measured: Objectives and Key Results (OKRs)   143
- Put It in Writing, Sign a Contract   146
- Benefits of the OKR System   148
- Differing Perspectives on Setting and Reaching Goals   152

Chapter Six
Innovate on Demand—Exactly What Is Worth Writing on the White Board?   157

- What Is SIT?   160
- The Five Templates   161
- The Closed World   165
- Changing The Closed World   166
- Getting Diabetes Medicine to China   167
- What Makes an Idea Creative?   168
- What are the Benefits of a Challenge?   169
- Every Challenge Is an Opportunity   171

Put It in Writing	172
Applying The SIT Process	173

Chapter Seven
Holding Effective Meetings — 187

Creating Safe Meetings	188
A Blueprint for Leading Effective Meetings	189
Preventing Fear-Ridden Meetings	202
Checking For Understanding	202
Offering Help	203
Innovating Your Meetings	203

Epilogue	**205**
Acknowledgements	**207**

Preface

Think back to a recent dispute you had with a friend or coworker. Perhaps you disagreed over the details of a conversation, or you thought you paid them back for money they laid out, but they remember otherwise. Perhaps they agreed to pay you to do a job, you completed the job, but there then was a disagreement over the scope of work. All these scenarios share one factor: memory. According to the Child Mind Institute, "working memory is an executive function that plays a major role in how we process, use and remember information on a daily basis."[1] We rely on our memory to learn and retain information and then recall it later. And herein lies the problem: Even when a group of people share the same experience, their memories of it may differ. This might be due to a variety of factors, including our physiology, perspective and life experience.

If you have already had negative experiences working with someone, you will be more on guard and will naturally seek proof to back up your own narrative. On the flipside, if your feelings are already positive, you're likely to see the narrative from a more positive perspective. The trouble is that when we are trying to resolve a problem, each of us inevitably remembers the scenario differently. The end result may be a conflict that cannot be resolved, even if compromise of some sort can be achieved.

---

[1] https://childmind.org/article/what-is-working-memory/.

Now imagine that as soon as an agreement or decision is reached, a written summary is sent, reviewed and agreed upon. Everyone at the table is on the same page about the money that will be laid out, any pay-back schedule, the exact scope of work and the fees to be paid. Clarity at every stage of a project—or a company's business—not only ensures healthy communication, it is vital to its success.

Over the past 20 years, I have been active in both the profit and not-for-profit sectors, as an employee, a manager and consultant. Almost every day I come across a challenge that could have been avoided with proper documentation. In fact, since I am bold by nature, I don't have a problem making the following statement—and I hope this book will convince you that I am correct!—80% of problems arise because no one can accurately remember the conversation that took place when we were making key decisions. The "he said, she said" game might be entertaining (or heart-breaking), but it's a waste of time and avoidable. As an aside, the same applies to family issues. No more fighting about whether or not someone said they'll take out the trash. Just make a note of it, and problems will be avoided later.

The scary part is that one disagreement often leads to the next. Friendships have ended and family ties have been severed over financial disputes. People have quit their jobs over heated, team arguments. Marriages have ended. How unfortunate that so many of these catastrophes could have been avoided.

In addition to avoiding future disputes, documentation offers other benefits. These can include increased goal-attainment and accountability, enhanced employee engagement and increased productivity. Enumerating all of these benefits only begs the question. Putting things in writing seems like a simple task and is obviously beneficial. So why don't we do it? Because...drumroll, please!...We are lazy. Or overwhelmingly busy, like the CEO who's constantly on the run and feels he is too busy to document. And the truth is, much of the time it isn't necessary to have things documented. Until it is. Conversations or meetings that happen when the relationship is strong—the deal seems straightforward and the terms are clear—don't seem to require documentation. But if you haven't documented any decisions made, then down the line, when the going can get tough, it is too late.

The idea is simple: Just write it down. Unfortunately, too often we don't. The idea of this book might seem simple, but clearly it isn't.

The topics in this book all focus on one or another aspect of doing business, demonstrating that each is best handled by taking the time to document. From setting goals to brainstorming to a host of HR issues, this book aims to leave no stone unturned.

WHO IS THIS BOOK FOR?

Until now, most HR books have been written by HR professionals and those with a legal background. I find that these books, although adored by their authors, are largely despised by regular employees. The odds are that if you have been hired to do a job that doesn't involve enforcing regulations, you aren't interested in hearing about more rules for the sake of rules. You don't understand why all these formalities are set in place, so when they are announced, your eyes glaze over. You basically ignore what is being taught, hoping you won't get caught committing any infractions. And when you do get reprimanded, you assure your boss that you'll do better, if only to get the HR payroll officer off your back.

I want to clarify that I am not an HR expert. And I'm okay with that, because I'm not here to turn you into an HR guru. I'm here to save you from disaster later, and, in the process, make your job easier.

Thanks to *Put It in Writing*, you now have a tool in your hand that is key to doing just that. Read it yourself and share it with your team. My hope is that by the end of this book, you begin to smile when someone says to put something in writing. Okay, maybe not a huge smile, but at least not an eye roll.

HOW THE BOOK WORKS

This book is not intended to make you into the one taking the minutes at every meeting. Instead, it can be used to help you in a few different ways:

- Provide a written record of conversations to have clarity later, if necessary
- Document projects and assignments for the sake of accountability
- Preparing properly for, and run, meetings
- Physically write out key aspects of the brainstorming process that emerge during a meeting or conversation, to ensure that innovation is being maximized

There are two parts to this book. Part one includes work situations where documentation is necessary, from hiring and firing to creating contracts and making policy exceptions. And it explains when documentation is *not* necessary. The second part includes such topics as setting and reaching goals, innovation and holding effective meetings and where documentation is a part of the process. You'll find they require more introduction and context.

Throughout the book you will find real-life anecdotes—called "STORIES" here—contributed by colleagues, clients and friends, and each illustrating what really happens when documentation is not handled properly. I think they add an important dose of reality to what might otherwise feel like a lot of warnings about hypothetical situations. I am deeply grateful for each one. Please note that story details and the names in each story have been changed to protect the identity of the contributors.

Also included at the end of some chapters are additional resources—toolkits and checklists, for instance—valuable tools for managing your business effectively.

My hope is that you'll find this book easy to read and, more importantly, easy to implement, and commits you to sending more follow-up emails and texts, to keeping expectations high and discord low. Whether it's hiring a painter for a small job or launching a start-up, commit to documenting. Because that's how you can help prevent 80% of the problems that typically plague most businesses.

PART I

CHAPTER ONE

The Basics of Documentation

Let's begin by looking at a number of business conflicts that can arise when written documentation is omitted or incomplete. Neither a promise of salary raises, nor a donation to a charity or a commitment to help with a project, is binding without the proper paperwork. "He said, she said" games take over when both parties to an agreement are holding on to conversations from two years past, even as they are grasping to remember the details. Even if one party insists that they are correct, even if a second person gives verbal consent, the agreement is unlikely to hold up. It's hard to reach an agreement when verbal promises can be read with different inflections, so just imagine when there's no backup at all.

That being said, here's a brief overview of the times when HR and Accounting would say that having proper documentation can be extremely valuable.

- **Legal protection**

    Documentation can be useful as evidence in disputes with employees, clients and vendors, as well as to prevent theft, fraud and mistaken charges.

- **Accountability**

    Documenting goals and upholding standards allow teams to track performance, measure progress and make data-driven decisions.

- **Minimizing waste**

    Creating standard operating procedures and documenting processes enable involved parties to pay attention and improve current business practices.

- **Project Management**

    Writing down goals, expectations, next steps and accountabilities for staff reduces ambiguity and leads to higher productivity.

- **Accurate Finances**

    Physically writing out, as supposed to estimating, all expenses and revenue provides us with the hard facts for determining whether a program or project is making money. It also provides for a smoother accounting process.

Before I go a bit deeper, I know what you are thinking: "Put everything in writing?? That's literally ridiculous. I'd be writing the entire day! Do you know how many meetings I have…?"

So, I want to clarify two things:

1. No, I don't mean literally everything.
2. The issues are always the times you didn't document.

THE BASICS OF DOCUMENTATION

So how do you know if you *really* must document? On the one hand, we can't write everything. On the other hand, whatever we don't document can become a problem later.

Here's my handy guide for determining when to document:

1. Use your brain. No, you don't have to be the secretary at every meeting and document when your employee blew their nose.

2. Take the time to ask yourself what the key takeaways are from every conversation. Then think: If any of this is not documented, can it possibly be harmful later?

3. If the answer is yes to the second question, document. If the answer is no, don't.

And to clarify, when I say document, I do not mean that you need a formal system or a cumbersome process. Yes, sometimes, you need to write a formal email to emphasize the seriousness of an issue. Mostly, however, a few bullet points (even in a text) should be fine. The key here is documentation, not formalities. I really can't stress enough how important this is. The difference between doing it and not doing it can cost you hundreds of hours of time, tons of aggravation and millions of dollars in settlements.

Tools like Fatham, Otter.ai and MeetGeek, are more formal systems for those who prefer "meeting assistants" that can record and transcribe your Zoom, Google Meet and Microsoft Teams calls automatically, and send the record or transcription to participants. Now that we live in the world of AI, utilizing these tools can be a game changer. Setting them to record automatically ensures that you have back-up for every one of these meetings.

Another key point is not just to document, but to document as soon as possible. It is best to document when the information is fresh in your mind so you can be as accurate as possible. There are also times when you need to document for your own protection, or to avoid legal issues later. In this case, as well, please document the situation immediately.

 **Story**

Michelle owns a Montessori middle school and sent 40 students and eight teachers, including Mr. Jones, on a boat ride for a class trip. Everyone on the boat was wearing life jackets and although it was a clear day, the water was quite frigid. One 8th grader, Carter, was a little too near the side of the boat, and leaned over to feel the water temperature. As he reached further still and went up on his tiptoes, Mr. Jones saw what was happening. He assessed the situation and quickly grabbed Carter by the back of his pants and reeled him to safety. As the kids gathered around, Carter thanked Mr. Jones. Acting correctly, Mr. Jones immediately emailed Michelle, the school's owner, letting her know what happened, what action he took, and who witnessed it. In this way, if Carter ever accused Mr. Jones of touching him inappropriately, Mr. Jones had all the backup he would need.

Now let's return to the list of issues HR would pinpoint as situations where documentation would be advisable.

LEGAL PROTECTION

Although the word legal often sounds scary, I am using it to cover many areas, specifically those that potentially involve financial implications. These can include hiring and firing, salary/bonus changes and expectations, contracts, expense reimbursement, paid time off, policies (harassment, discrimination), and sponsorship/donation pledges.

Hiring

You meet Aron for the first time in an interview and he seems to be the perfect candidate. You get to the salary discussion and throw out some vague numbers, reference a moving package and remote work, as well as the potential to move up in the company over time. Of course, Aron is thrilled. He just heard you say that he'll be the CEO within three years and be able to work fully remote from Cancun. You aren't sure why he looks like he just won the jackpot but assume it's because he's just relieved to get hired in this tight job market. You send out a basic contract, including the salary offer, but make no mention of the other promises. Everything starts off great until he sends you an invoice—$9,500 for moving. That's strange: He only moved one state over and said it was just him and his dog. You ask him for an itemized receipt from the moving company and he provides it. It includes the full packing package, plus an extra $1,000 to move his baby grand piano. You're truly in shock, but aren't really sure what to do. Aron has a lot of potential, so you sheepishly shell out the money, feeling resentful but having no way to avoid making the payment.

Two months later, Aron comes to you to confirm you're okay if he starts working from home on Fridays and Mondays, as this way he can have more travel flexibility and be "all in" on Tuesday, Wednesday and Thursday. You're completely taken aback. You just finally got everyone off of remote work, and he has the audacity to ask for a four-day weekend—every week, no less?!? You invite him in for a conversation and tell him that you can't grant his request. He gets very angry and says you promised him remote work. You vaguely remember the conversation and say that you remember discussing remote work but definitely didn't promise two days remote each week. Well, Aron says he remembers the conversation clearly, that you seemed to have no problem with remote work. He threatens to get HR involved. You calm him down and ask him to compromise. You settle on Fridays and every other Monday as remote days. He walks out still upset, but pacified, and you crunch to the floor, not knowing what you will tell your other employees... This story goes on and on. But it could have been avoided.

In another case, Sheila is hired to work as a non-profit program director. Before accepting the job, one of the big negotiation points was childcare. As part of her job, Sheila would need to work evening hours and she wasn't interested in expending additional expenses for this work, as the salary wasn't exactly high. The hiring employer, Rick, agrees that he would "cover childcare," as written in her contract. You can imagine Rick's surprise when he learned that he was expected to cover the $30,000 au pair bill. "That's insane," Rick says. "I meant we would cover babysitting for your

💬 Story

Seth worked at a restaurant every summer, making an extra $7,000 annually to help cover his year-round expenses. One year, a manager asked Seth if he could start helping out on Wednesdays, normally his day off, and that he'd receive a bonus in exchange, if he agreed. By now you know where this is going. Nothing was put in writing. Seth was extremely upset when at the end of the summer he received $7,500—only $500 over his normal take-in each summer. Seth had worked an extra 15 hours of time, and hoped to make at least an extra $1,100. With nothing in writing, and only a vague promise of a bonus, Seth was stuck nursing his loss.

In another situation, Seth took on additional work for a non-profit fundraising project, and was once again promised a bonus. And again the bonus was not clearly documented. At the end of the year-long project, the non-profit did not meet their fundraising goal, as they did not receive the grant they submitted to fund it. Despite all the work Seth did, he never received his bonus. Without the grant it was counting on, the non-profit didn't have enough money to pay him.

In a third story, poor Seth, being extremely handy, was often called on to do small projects in the community. This time, a school called him for help with an AV project. Seth assumed they would pay the $500 they had paid for the same project the previous year, so he never discussed price, and obviously had nothing documented. When he finished the job, he never received payment, so he followed up a week later asking for his check. After the school hemmed and hawed, Seth eventually realized that when they asked for help, they assumed it was pro bono.

(Footnote: Seth is working on putting better strategies in place to avoid these situations in the future.)

CONTRACTS

As expectations are the key to disappointment, clear contracts can prevent business disputes and misunderstandings. They help establish clear expectations, reduce ambiguity and ensure all parties involved understand their obligations. Without them, you can be robbed of your hard-earned money, the time you spent and even your reputation. Writing and reviewing contracts are key to ensuring that disputes are settled properly.

 Story

Company Q hired a coach bus to take their team on a two-day trip to the mountains. There would be four stops on the trip. The first day was a trip to the beach and then to the hotel; the second day would be a stop for an incredible hiking experience, followed by a return to the office. The trip started without a hitch, but when day two rolled around, instead of taking the group on the hike, the driver mistakenly took them back to the beach they'd gone to the day before. Everyone was obviously annoyed, and the trip organizers had to spend extra money to distract the team from this unfortunate turn of events. The next day, in the office, the organizers reached out to the bus company, knowing that they were 100% right about what had happened the day before. In addition, they had the contract. Upon review of the contract after the trip, they were notified that they would receive only a partial credit for future bus company use. Now, not only did they have a partially ruined trip, but they had been sucked into using the same company again.

Refunds can become a major mess if not properly documented. You must state not only the price but what happens when a refund is requested. Often people are afraid to include a refund clause because they worry that mentioning the word refund will plant ideas in people's heads: Maybe if refunds are not discussed in advance, they won't be asked about them later. Unfortunately, this is not reality. Refunds are inevitable, due to unforeseen circumstances or just because the customer changed their mind. Nevertheless, make sure your contract includes what happens in case a refund is needed. Consider the following questions:

A. Are you offering a refund at all? What about in the case of emergencies?

B. If you are offering a refund, does it matter when the requests are made? Is it the same refund amount if it is requested in advance? What happens if someone requests it within 24 hours, after you've already spent a lot of money?

C. Does the reason for the refund matter, or do you refund regardless of whether the reason is acceptable?

D. What about someone who wants only a partial refund? On what grounds do you offer it?

Please state the refund policy clearly on your website and/or in the contract. It can save you a lot of financial aggravation.

Story

Dan had a side hustle offering photography sessions for families. He received a call from the Johnsons and arranged to meet them on a Sunday at the park. They agreed on the price of $150 for a 30-minute shoot. It all went very well and the Johnsons were thrilled. They asked when Dan would send the final pictures and he responded that they would be sent within three days. Three days later, Dan promptly emailed over the final pictures. The Johnsons loved them and asked when they would receive the printed copies. Dan was taken aback as he had never included prints in the price. The Johnsons were also taken aback, as they also wouldn't have paid $150 for just digital prints. They asked for a refund of $75 or 30 assorted prints. Since Dan didn't have a refund policy in place, he ended up refunding half the money. He walked away extremely frustrated.

As Dan continued his side hustle, he did a small editing job for a client. The fee was $600 and the client agreed to pay it. After finishing the job, the client sent $25 and said he couldn't pay the entire amount at once. He said he could pay $25 a month over time. Because Dan didn't have the payment terms in writing he was stuck accepting $25 a month over two years—never mind the cost of inflation. Although it was a small amount, Dan learned this lesson the hard way.

Story

Mary ran a camp every summer for the local community. Although the camp wasn't very large, it brought in significant income for her as overhead was extremely low. Here are three unfortunate situations that Mary experienced, all because of lack of tracking and contracts.

In her first summer, Mary kept track of all registrants and payments, although she did it on paper. To her chagrin, her papers got ruined in the rain and she was left with zero records. She didn't know who registered, how much they paid...It was definitely a learning opportunity.

Early on, Mary committed to being super-organized. She reached out to families well in advance so she could get a sense of her numbers and could save money on rush-shipping materials. Many parents responded to her calls and she began purchasing. As the summer approached, Mary reached back out to the families to collect payment. Although some of them complied, many of them responded that their plans had changed and they were no longer sending their kids. Mary was extremely frustrated but had no ammunition. She was stuck with the materials she'd ordered and needed to spend a lot more time recouping her losses and recruiting more campers.

One summer, Mary took payments via the Zelle payment app. Parents would use Zelle to send money directly to her bank account and Mary would do the accounting. This summer, in particular, Mary had a large number of registrants and many of them Zelled at the same time. If you are not familiar with the app, Zelle works via bank transfer from one account to another. There is room to write a note so the recipient knows what the money is being sent for, but many people do not use this feature. What that means is that many times payments come in with no name and are not connected to a particular camper. Mary had been extremely busy and by the time she sat down to deal with the accounting, her bank account was an absolute mess. It was a business account, which was helpful, but she had a lot of payments, many for different amounts, and she had no idea how to figure out what was from whom. To her embarrassment, she needed to reach out to multiple families to confirm that they paid, on what day and the amount paid. It definitely was a learning experience.

It is also extremely important to state the payment terms. When do you need the payment collected? Before the work starts? 50% up front and 50% after it's complete? Whatever you decide, it must be clearly stated in writing. Even more importantly, you must be particularly careful not to do the work before receiving payment. Otherwise, you may end up working and not being compensated. To illustrate this, I have included a variety of stories. Unfortunately, there are many.

💬 Story

Leslie was a life coach who charged $500 per session. Most clients signed up for a three-month package (12 sessions) for a discounted price of $5,500. Her meetings with Max started out well, at least she thought so, even though Max wasn't exactly an easy client to work with. He repeatedly diverted the conversations, bringing up irrelevant topics that wasted time. Two weeks in, Max shared that he felt that the sessions weren't progressing quickly enough and he wasn't sure he wanted to continue. Leslie shared that it was hard to progress quickly as he kept diverting the conversation. Max agreed to stay more focused the next week and Leslie made it her business to keep Max very much on task. At the end of the third session, Max said that he was much happier. He asked for two extra sessions to compensate for the first two weaker sessions. Leslie wasn't sure what to do as Max was well-connected in the business world. She ended up giving in as she had no clear policy for this kind of case. The three months (plus two extra sessions) ended on a great note, but until this day, Leslie regrets that she wasn't more firm.

⌬ Story

A travel agent, Simon booked mostly international trips. He could make some money on flights, but the higher commission came when he was booking hotels. As such, if someone reached out to book flights only, he had a higher fee ($100 per ticket), while that fee was lowered when it was coupled with hotel bookings. (The hotel would pay the commission.) One day, the Marx family reached out and asked for four international tickets totaling $8,500. While Simon normally charged both the airfare fee and his fees on the same card, the Marx family asked if they could pay them on different cards. They gave him the credit card to cover the $8,500 over the phone, which Simon processed. The family said that they would call the next day with a different card.

A little backstory: Simon, with their approval, had booked their flights with a stopover in Europe of close to three hours. After the flights were booked, the Marx family decided the stopover was too short, and called the airline directly to change their tickets to a longer stopover. Simon saw what they did and reached out to tell them that the new flight was often delayed and recommended that they switch their flights again, which they did. Simon also asked for his $400 fee. The Marx family refused to pay, saying that they not only had to do all the leg work switching the flight—because they didn't like the stopover—but they also had to pay processing fees for doing it over the phone. Simon argued back that they had agreed to the original flight, and he could have switched the flight for them if they had asked. He felt he still deserved payment for his time, despite their decision to change their flight. With no policy in writing and no recourse, Simon was left with a lot of frustration.

A few months earlier, Simon had another incident. A mother and father, also a family friend, decided to ask Simon to book a surprise trip to visit their son before he enlisted in the army. The son had a week off before leaving, so they thought it would be the perfect time to visit. A few days after booking, their son found out what they were planning and apologized: He was already going on another trip with his friends and wouldn't be around. The parents were devastated and realized they would be forfeiting their no-refund tickets. Simon, afraid they would ask for a refund (they were family friends), ended up calling the son directly, explaining the situation and convincing him to back out of the trip with his friends, which he did. Everyone lived happily ever after, but Simon narrowly avoided an uncomfortable, expensive situation.

💬 Story

Marsha had her first baby a short time after being married. She and her husband Ben were ecstatic. They hired a baby photographer, who promised that the photos would be ready within two days of the photo shoot. Although skeptical, Marsha paid $350 up front. The shoot happened on a Wednesday. Come Friday, the pictures were nowhere to be seen. Marsha and Ben reached out countless times over the next two months and still never saw the pictures. Furthermore, the photographer blocked Marsha on social media so she couldn't follow up via those channels. Only after threatening to sue her, and getting multiple parties involved, did they see the pictures (which weren't good), two months after the original shoot. With nothing in writing, and full payment in advance, there was nothing more Marsha or Ben could do.

💬 Story

Brian and his wife Leora rented an apartment for three years. They had a good relationship with the landlord and let him know three months in advance that they would be moving out, as per the contract. After they moved out, the landlord sent them a bill for $2,500 to cover additional damages. Shocked, they asked for the list, which the landlord provided. The list included miniscule things they felt should have been overlooked. As for the larger items, they felt that had they known about them prior to moving out, they would have taken care of them themselves. After many calls and emails back and forth, they eventually settled on $1,250. That amount could have been avoided if Brian and Leora had taken more time studying their move-in contract three years prior, as well as asked the landlord for a move-out list detailing what he expected from them. With that list in hand, they would have known exactly what items they could fix, and what they would need to pay for.

 Story

Levi took a part-time clergy job with a non-profit. As part of his role, he committed to lead a one-hour prayer service at 7:30 a.m. Monday through Friday, for which he would be compensated $10,000. Everything was going very well. The non-profit was happy. Levi was happy. Then, mid-year, the non-profit decided to switch their prayer time, first to 7 a.m. and then to 6:30 a.m. Levi did try to make it work at first, but it was too trying with his young family at home. He kept asking them to switch it back, as he had committed to a 7:30 a.m. start. The non-profit wouldn't acquiesce, nor did they want to continue paying him, as he could no longer make the new service time. Although his commitment to lead the prayer service was documented in the contract, the *start* of the prayer time was not. In the end, because of the strong relationship Levi had with the non-profit, it did agree to continue payment until the end of the year. Levi was lucky, but the lesson is still the same: Get it in writing.

Be extremely diligent when purchasing or leasing cars for your business. Car dealerships are notorious for advertising pricing and then when a potential customer comes to the lot, the dealer "happens" to mention a variety of hidden fees that weren't included in the ad. Be diligent and ask for everything in writing to make sure you are not paying inflated pricing that you never agreed to.

EXPENSE REIMBURSEMENT

Although this was touched upon above, there are many gray areas where the issue of reimbursing expenses can get uncomfortable. First, when an employee travels for work, what exactly is covered? First-class travel? Business? Coach? What about food? First-class restaurants three times a day? Does the company reimburse for miles driven? Pay for gas? Pay for their cellphone? Reimburse for hosting clients? What level of client meetings are covered? Coffee?

Drinks? Full meals? How about professional development workshops? What workshops are covered? How about a less formal one? Who keeps the credit-card miles and points for flights and hotels? The list does go on and on. But the point is the same: Put everything in writing. If you do it *before* the hire, amazing. If things come up on the job, do it then. It's never too late to avoid mistakes.

 **Story**

Non-profit M was constantly paying for taxis for their employees to run programs. The expenses were getting out of hand, so they decided to curb spending for an upcoming, large-scale program. They emailed and WhatsApped all staff, letting them know that taxi reimbursements would only be made if a taxi was utilized by a group of four staff members simultaneously. This would prevent waste—and keep employees from ordering 10 taxis from the same address just five minutes apart. Although some staff forgot and ordered taxis, their reimbursement requests were rejected, and those rejection emails were sent together with the original email as back-up. Some of those violators were annoyed, but had only themselves to blame.

The following story illustrates a different angle, when a medical patient hides the fact that they've received reimbursements, despite the policy being in writing. Read on.

💬 Story

Michael was the director of a nursing rehabilitation facility. One day, Dan arrived after surgery and needed to stay for three months. Here's the background: when someone with Medicaid requires long-term care, Medicaid covers part of the cost, while Social Security pays an additional portion. That Social Security check is supposed to go directly to the facility. In some cases, however, it's mailed to the patient's home instead. In those situations, the patient is responsible for turning the funds over to the facility. Unfortunately, some patients claim they never received the check, leaving the facility unable to prove otherwise. In Dan's case, Michael took the matter to court. The facility won—but they could just as easily have lost. The lesson: Even if policies are written down, they must be signed. In this case, there was an admission form, but the facility wasn't on top of getting the signatures, and they were often skipped. When policies are especially critical, you must double-check to see that they're signed, as well as understood verbally. This way, the information is clearly comprehended and documented.

POLICIES

The topic of policies is a broad one, and can cover anything from harassment and discrimination to conduct and behavior, from environmental sustainability to emergency response and data compliance. What's key here is that everything be documented. This ensures that expectations are clear and, even more importantly, reviewed, as we know that people often don't read what they sign. A company can have a long list of policies that no one knows anything about, as well as a long list that is vaguely acknowledged and each employee interprets differently. The magic solution is documented policies that are reviewed biannually.

 Story

An after-school non-profit for youth had primarily white children in attendance, for no reason other than its location. One summer, a black family registered their child, who was welcomed to the program. One Wednesday, their daughter was made fun of, and although the program dealt meaningfully with the situation, and even called the parents to let them know what had occurred, the parents were unhappy and pulled their daughter from the program. There hadn't been a racism policy previously, as it hadn't been relevant, and the parents felt that the current bullying policy hadn't been substantial enough. Thankfully, after the school year, the girl's parents sat down with the director and helped him draft a policy for the upcoming school year so that the situation could be avoided in the future.

An additional reason to have policies in place is to ensure psychological safety for all employees. All staff must know that their employer will have their back if they are ever feeling justifiably uncomfortable. They should feel safe speaking up when things don't feel right, and they should be able to trust the policies in place to uphold a safe workplace. No matter a person's race, color, religion, gender and national origin, all people need to feel safe at all times. No one should fear termination due to any factors unrelated to work.

💬 Story

Asher had some tough shoes to fill in his new job, as was made clear to him from day one. As soon as he was hired to run the college's career counseling office, Jill, an undergraduate at the college, had it in for him. Asher had replaced Jill's best friend as the director of the office, and she was very bitter about it. In order to get others on the same page as her, Jill would talk to anyone about how bad Asher was. Asher never spoke to his manager about it, as he kept brushing it off, not wanting to seem like a baby who couldn't hold his own. Then one day, Jill found the perfect ammunition. She saw Asher making a U-turn with college students in the car. Even though the U-turn was legal, Jill knew it was time to get her revenge. She wrote a livid email to Asher's manager about how irresponsible Asher was, and about the U-turn she'd witnessed him making. She also demanded the complaint be escalated further. Asher's manager scheduled a meeting with him and reprimanded him for the incident. At that point, Asher finally opened up and explained the whole situation and the bullying that had been going on. When his manager asked Asher why he hadn't reported it until then, Asher said he'd just shrugged it off.

Now, however, Asher wasn't sure what to do. Jill had sent an email in writing and requested a review of the employee handbook to see all the potential violations Asher had violated. His manager told Asher not to respond to Jill in writing, that he would personally deal with the situation. Just two hours later, Jill sent another email with a copy of the handbook, highlighting and underlining all of Asher "egregious" violations. Two hours after that, she sent a third email, this time demanding that if Asher didn't respond ASAP, she would reach out to the president of the college. Early the next morning, Jill sent a final email calling for Asher's termination and copied the college president.

At that point, Asher's manager called Jill. He told her in no uncertain terms that she would not be allowed to contact Asher, and that if she did, there would be serious consequences, perhaps even jeopardizing her ability to graduate with her peers. He then sent a follow-up email to Jill, copying the president, to make sure everything was documented. Jill eventually dropped her witch hunt and Asher was able to breathe easily.

Lessons of the story:

- Document early, as soon as you can.

- Make sure your employees know and follow company policies.

- Make sure that your staff members feel safe and know you have their back.

Paid Time Off

PTO can work along the same lines as expense reimbursements. How many vacation and sick days does an employee get? If they don't use them, can they roll them over to the next year? Buy them out? Can they take vacation whenever they want, or do the days need to be approved by a manager? What happens when an employee takes more days than are available to them? Again, conflicts can be avoided with proper documentation.

 Story

School E had been clear about their vacation policy. All teachers received 10 vacation days per year and could only take them during certain seasons. Additionally, they received five paid, sick days that could be used as needed. There had never been any problems until one teacher requested to receive payment for unused sick days, claiming that she should be incentivized to get coverage for her kids when they are sick, so that she could be fully present for her students. Since there had been no previous policy in place, the school board needed to vote on the matter. They ultimately decided to adopt the policy and included it in future handbooks.

 Story

A billing company has 50 employees. The company's policy is that all full-time employees receive two weeks' paid vacation days, while all part-time employees receive one week. Claire was a very committed worker and didn't have a family of her own. She almost never took off, figuring she'd eventually cash in the unused days. One day, after 10 years at the company, Claire went in to ask her supervisor, Jon, how to take her five months' paid vacation.

Flabbergasted, Jon had no idea what she was referring to. She shared that she had been saving up her vacation days for 10 years and wanted to take them all at once to take a cruise around the world. Never having been asked that before, and not having an accrual policy in place, Jon said he'd need to research the matter and get back to her. After consulting with senior staff in the company and realizing they didn't have a proper policy in place, Jon had a follow-up meeting with Claire. He said he understood her position, but that it would be extremely hard on the company to lose her for five months straight. They eventually compromised on a two-month cruise and a three-month cash payout. Rest assured, a new policy was put into place immediately.

Legal Deals

Historically a handshake may have signified the closing of a business deal, but it is essentially useless now. Unless there is written documentation, there's no proof whether it's a "deal or no deal." Even during due diligence, the entire deal can be retracted. In order to ensure the deal goes through, be sure that you have filled out all necessary legal paperwork.

 **Story**

Jim found the perfect building to purchase for his bike-repair business. It was in a great location and had enough room to fix about 25 motorcycles at once, his average workload. He knew the seller from high school and was excited to go ahead with the purchase. They shook hands and even went out for drinks. Then, the night before the sale, Jim got a call from the seller's agent that the sale had fallen through and the seller had gone with a different buyer, one who was offering $35,000 over list price. Shocked that his so-called friend would do such a thing, but even more upset that he wasn't called directly, Jim didn't know what to do. And that was perfect, because there wasn't anything to do. He had nothing in writing to even use as evidence, nor had he made a deposit on the property. Lesson learned: Always put deals in writing.

There can even be legal problems once the establishment of a new business has been finalized. Here's a special caveat about going into business with friends: Dealing with friends is precisely when you may assume you have the least need for legal documentation, and that mistake can come back to haunt you.

💬 Story

Jill and Donna had been friends since childhood, always dreaming up their next business ideas together. When they stayed friends through college and into adulthood, it only seemed natural that they would go into business together. They started an online resale business. Donna, who was great at thrifting, would go from store to store buying up, bargaining, photographing and posting pictures, and Jill would take care of the marketing, sales, shipping and finances. They would evenly split the money generated from sales. The two of them invested in a small warehouse, each contributing $50,000 in seed money. And Donna laid out a lot of money for store purchases. Unfortunately, Jill's husband's health took a turn for the worse, and Jill had to take a step back to care for him. At that point, Donna found herself at a crossroads: She had a lot of merchandise she didn't know what to do with, and she couldn't even talk to Jill about it, as her friend was completely overwhelmed. Should Donna hire someone? Arrange for a garage sale and sell everything? Since they had never hired a lawyer or drafted an agreement, Donna was really confused. They had made all the decisions about their business together. If Jill didn't agree with Donna's decisions later, what would she do? Donna eventually decided to just provide Jill with updates:

Update 1: I don't want to bother you. Just letting you know, I think we should hire a liquidation company to sell off all the merchandise. They would keep 50% of the profits and they're guaranteeing $25,000. If I don't hear from you by Friday, I'll assume you're okay with it.

Update 2: I found a serious buyer for the warehouse. We can sell it for full-cost value. If I don't hear from you, I'll sell it by Tuesday.

In the end, Jill's husband recovered, and she was okay with Donna's decisions. But the process was extremely stressful and that could have been avoided.

Intellectual Property

If you have any product concepts, ideas, process procedures or improvements that you don't want your employees to pursue if and when they eventually leave your company, then please make sure to document ownership of it. Trademark when necessary, but even placing your logo/watermark on every sheet and asking your employees to sign non-compete/non-disclosure forms, when necessary, can go a long way toward avoiding disputes later.

Sponsorship/Donation Pledges

Ah... I've decided to save the best for last. Not that this topic is more important than the others, but the stories are unfortunately endless. In essence, every pledge or event sponsorship should be documented, regardless of when it is made.

If you receive the donation on the spot, document it as received. If you receive a pledge for it, document that, as well as document again after it was received.

But where do you document it? Are your own internal notes useful? And the answer is... another drumroll, please... *NO*. As soon as you receive the commitment, send an email/text/WhatsApp message (or other appropriate form of communication), thanking them for their pledge and specifying the *EXACT* amount of the pledge. Yes, email is best. But if you always communicate with this funder over text, text might need to suffice. I also include the following line after every important piece of communication: "If I don't hear back from you within [24/48/72 hours...], I will assume that you agree to the contents of this email."

This one sentence has proven to be a game changer for me. I receive responses more quickly, and if there is any miscommunication, it can be cleared up right away. It is a bit bold, but the negative repercussions when not including it are just not worth the risk.

Let me share some unfortunate stories:

 Story

Organization C solicited a $45,000 donation from a donor and offered to make him the guest of honor at their upcoming dinner. He accepted, and the dinner went off without a hitch. After the dinner, the organization's CEO asked the donor to pay the pledge amount. The donor responded that $45,000 wasn't a "firm" commitment, but rather a "hopeful" one. Despite receiving an honor for a commitment that the CEO *knew* was "firm," the donor did not live up to his word. (As a side note, even more than getting it in writing, the donation should have been paid before the event happened.)

Story

Company Y was hosting their annual golf outing and had secured a sponsorship from the local bar for alcohol for the event. The bar committed to providing both the beer and the hard alcohol, and Company Y went to work promoting the bar in all their marketing material. The event went off seamlessly, and "cheers" were clinked by all, yet Company Y was surprised to receive a large bill for the alcohol. They approached the bar and asked why they were receiving an invoice for $5,500 when the bar had agreed to sponsor the beer and alcohol. The bar responded that it never would have agreed to that, and had only offered to sponsor the beer. Again, without everything in writing, Company Y was left with a hefty bill, in addition to a hangover.

💬 Story

Organization D solicited a bequest from a current donor. This donor's lifetime giving had exceeded $200,000, and he was more than happy to commit to a legacy gift. The non-profit celebrated the commitment with an announcement and even wrote an article about it in their annual magazine. But reality set in when the donor unfortunately passed away before the paperwork was ever finalized. The donor's children, who lived at a distance, didn't understand the importance of this non-profit to their father, and decided to donate a portion of his money to their charity of choice. Everything *should* have worked out, and not getting documentation promptly was a major set-back for the non-profit.

ACCOUNTABILITY AND DRIVING SALES AND RECRUITMENT

Let's move on to a broader topic. A key reason to document just about everything is accountability. Both physically writing down goals and upholding standards allow teams to track performance, measure progress and make data-driven decisions. It is also extremely helpful for project-management purposes, as it allows for clear requirements, tracking progress, and measuring results. In fact, data suggests that clearly setting expectations in writing significantly increases the likelihood of achieving desired outcomes, with studies indicating that individuals who document their goals are 42% more likely to achieve them. Additionally, research by psychology professor Dr. Gail Matthews demonstrates that people who write down their goals are significantly more likely to achieve them, compared to those who only think about them.[2]

Objectives and Key Results (OKRs) provide a framework for setting goals. Developed by Intel ex-CEO Andy Grove, it is key in establishing accountability. Writing down an organization's annual objective creates clarity and a benchmark for the team. Even for smaller projects, such as putting on conferences or securing a large client, documentation allows us to track progress. Knowing that only 150 attendees have registered for the event, when last year at the same time we had secured 180, tells us we need to increase

---

[2] "Dr. Matthews' study delved into the psychology of goal setting and achievement. Her findings revealed a striking statistic: individuals who commit their goals to paper are 33-42% more likely to achieve them compared to those who merely conceptualize their goals." https://www.davron.net/the-science-behind-goal-achievement/.

our marketing. Looking at the list from last year's attendance sheet also tells us who needs to be targeted directly for recruitment. By the way, there will be a lot more about OKRs in a later chapter!

Note: I have often organized the same fundraising event year after year. I constantly use lists and data to track attendees based on registration by date and sponsorship pledges by date. This has allowed me to be hyper-aware of the progress we are making and helps guide many of the fundraising committee's decisions.

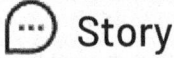 Story

Business F hired All Star Catering for their upcoming conference. They worked together on a meal-by-meal menu and agreed on a price. They received an invoice, promptly paid the 50% deposit, and looked forward to the event. As you might have predicted, they were far from impressed by the catering actually provided for the event. Here are some surprises they experienced:

- The salad bar with 10 vegetables became the salad bar with five fresh and five canned vegetables.
- The ice cream bar was all sherbert.
- The same bread rolls were served three times.
- The meat portions were extremely small.

- The caterer used the last meal as an opportunity to re-serve some of their leftovers.

After the event they sat down with the caterer, who was awaiting final payment. The event organizers patiently went through the menu line by line, showing her the areas where she didn't deliver the promised level of service. They were able to compromise on a fair price, and the organizers went away knowing they wouldn't be hiring the caterer again but at least feeling that they were compensated. The meal-by-meal planning in advance allowed business F to hold the caterer accountable for areas where the product fell short of what was agreed upon.

Minimizing Waste

Creating and writing down standard operating procedures, known as SOPs, enables involved parties to pay attention and improve current procedures. Documenting spending habits can also save a tremendous amount of money.

Standard Operating Procedures (SOPs) are step-by-step instructions documenting systems and processes within a company. They ensure consistency and quality, as they document replicable instructions that allow a company to streamline operations. Without them, employees would step on each other's toes, as they all fumble to complete the same tasks. SOPs allow for a proper division of labor, minimizing productivity waste. By constantly reviewing procedures and focusing in on specific steps, SOPs allow space for improvements to be made.

💬 Story

Barbara was completely overwhelmed. Solopreneur gone business owner, the HR consultant had somehow ended up over her head. She had secured three new clients this particular month and was faced with the stark reality that she needed to do all the work *plus* keep up with business development. She knew she had to hire but didn't know where to start. The thought of taking time to teach someone everything they would need to know was completely overwhelming. Fortunately, Barbara had a business consultant who helped her calm down and start to document her SOPs. The consultant asked her a series of questions to get started: What do you do first? What needs to be done after that? How do you do it? What words do you use? What color shirt do you wear? Together, and with the help of AI, step-by-step guides and instructions were created, together with video tutorials. Once Barbara was armed with the protocols, she was able to hire contractors who could each tackle a percentage of the scope of work. The job descriptions were simple to write and were niched down—narrowed in focus—so that only appropriate applicants applied for the job.

Documenting SOPs is critical when onboarding new employees. When processes and systems are documented, training is fairly simple. You only need to allocate staff to give over the information. But when that content is stored in different people's heads, and perhaps done differently by each person in the company, you have an onboarding nightmare. Do not forget to document training that was done in passing or in conversation. A quick follow-up email—"Here are the things we discussed today"—is a good idea. Even better, as soon as you realize you are in the middle of training, start recording it and email the recording afterward. That's a good way to avoid an employee claiming, "Oh, I didn't realize I needed to do that..."

The same holds true with telephone support. If you haven't documented a process for what exactly staff should do when customers call, how exactly to answer the phone, what to do when there's a problem, and so on, the culture you are trying to build melts away. Each person on the team needs to understand what they are doing and why and this information needs to be documented. The book *E-Myths Revisited* by Michael E. Gerber, founder of a business-skills training company, discusses this in depth.[3] Using a parable about the distraught owner of a pie shop who is ready to close the business, Gerber teaches emerging and frustrated entrepreneurs the key ingredients in running a successful business. Not only does the book stress the importance of each member of the team knowing their specific role, but every single role must also be documented and each person serving in

---

[3] Michael E. Gerber, *The E-Myth Revisited: A Guide to Starting a Business in a Productive and Successful Way*, Harper Business, 2004. ISBN-13 978-0887307287.

that role must sign a contract assuming responsibility for it. Although this might make logical sense, Gerber insists that this must be done even if the company has one employee who is serving in every role. That one employee must sign a contract for every single role he assumes. Then as he hires more people for specific jobs, he can relinquish some responsibilities as new employees sign a contract for their particular role. All this contractual work must be written down, documented and signed.

Additionally, take care to document customer complaints. Knowing when and how many times a person called to make a complaint, and documenting the takeaways from that conversation, can be extremely helpful in reaching a final resolution. This is true in conversations with problematic employees, as well. Tracking everything can only benefit you and your company in the future. Worse-case scenario, you lost the time it took to document.

The same can be said regarding budget planning and analysis. Does the following sound familiar? How many times have you organized an event or hosted a dinner or planned a trip, and thought you "didn't spend that much money", but when you sat down and actually counted up the charges, you get a sharp dose of reality? All those trips to Starbucks, and those Uber-Eat, Instacart and Amazon orders really added up. Before you knew it, your event that you thought cost $25,000 now ballooned to $35,000, your dinner cost $400 more than planned and your trip was $1,000 over budget.

 Story

James ran a wellness program at his mental health clinic. He was responsible for building opportunities for relaxation and self-care in the day-to-day schedule of his employees. With a $1,200 budget for the first month, James considered ordering a massage chair. He quickly realized it wasn't a worthwhile investment as only one person could use it at a time. He then considered buying some under-the-desk exercise equipment, but quickly vetoed that, too. Finally, he came up with a plan: Every Wednesday would be Wellness Wednesday, and he'd provide healthy snacks in the office, as well as giving out different merchandise—a logo'd water bottle, sports socks and even a drifit shirt or hoodie. He did some basic pricing but somehow ended up quite out of budget.

How did it happen, you ask? Well...

- He forgot to calculate rush-shipping on his merch order.
- He ordered some items from Costco, but then forgot what he ordered, and reordered similar items from Amazon.
- He ordered hundreds of drinks but forgot to calculate the bottle-deposit fee and tax.

Since he had spent $1,600 during the first month, he only had $800 to spend for the second month. He knew he needed to get back on track quickly. Here's how he stayed in budget:

- He wrote down every single charge and added up the totals every few days to manage spending:
  - He documented price quotes and compared them to past purchases.
  - He chose not to give out merchandise every month.
  - He offered raffle prizes that didn't cost the office anything—parking in the president's spot for a day and getting coffee with the CEO, for example.

Writing down what you do and how you do it, as well as tracking spending, will help to minimize waste. And as always, it's not enough to track it in your head. It must be put in writing! Seeing those numbers in black and white makes all the difference.

PROJECT MANAGEMENT

The term project management covers a variety of stages, from idea initiation to closing it up. The most valuable times for documentation in project management can include, but are not limited to, the following:

- During the project execution phase, when you are setting goals and expectations, delegating jobs and holding personnel accountable

- Hiring staff to execute the project, as you gather approval to hire and establish salary ranges

- When you're budgeting, including receiving approval to allocate money towards specific projects

Overseeing a project can be extremely taxing, especially when there are multiple cooks in the kitchen. What exacerbates the situation, though, is when different parties remember different conversations…differently. All you need is for one person to think of the budget as "the sky's the limit—so long as it makes the boss happy," while a second person thinks that the budget is "only an issue once the project takes longer than three months." Without clarity, in writing, everyone's assumptions remain just that.

Things that you definitely want in writing, ideally in a written thread, are:

1. **Goals of the project:** How is success defined? Is the important metric the number of people who attend the event, or the number of new clients gained? Is the metric an increase in employee retention or 5-star ratings on all surveys? What's key here is that the goals are written down and that there's a number attached to them, so they are measurable. (See above.) If a goal changes at a later time, that change must also be in writing and sent to all relevant parties.

2. **Tasks that need to get done:** List them out. On paper. What are the 10 things that need to happen to reach our goal?

3. **Allocation of jobs** required for the project: Next to each item, write the name of the person who is responsible for that one item. If you are the sole person responsible, write your name next to every item.

4. **Accountability:** At team meetings, review progress. If the team is losing focus, get everyone back on track. Reward success. Write down any adjustments and share those with the group. Review them again at the following meeting.

Document all these phases of a project, and you will have avoided much unnecessary stress.

Story

Small business T hoped to outsource some of its work to foreign workers. The plan was to get a few estimates from different staffing agencies and then choose one. After a few interviews, they realized that it would be more economical to handle the staffing themselves. Although they had never hired overseas staff directly, it was worth trying. The project was complicated, but because each person knew their role, everything went smoothly. They used a WhatsApp group. During each meeting, as soon as someone assumed responsibility for a task, the secretary noted it in the WhatsApp group. "Max will interview three people by Monday," for instance, or "Dave will research best overseas internet rates." By utilizing WhatsApp, a real-time platform where users can see and respond to everyone simultaneously, the number of "he said, she said" moments was drastically reduced.

At times, additional staff are needed when a business needs to execute a project. Although it is always key to have all salaries and benefits written down, in this case it is even more crucial. Because project execution can happen so quickly, the decision to hire someone could happen in a matter of minutes. If the project is time-sensitive, the hire must be pushed through almost instantaneously, and proper documentation is often missing. Moreover, sometimes the group will agree on a hire, but forget to go through the proper HR channels, because of the urgency of the hire. This creates legal problems later: What if someone was (irresponsibly) promised back pay for work that started before the hiring date? Or the job comes with some cushy, first-class flight options? Even though the process is rushed, you must make sure that every "promise" is documented. That way it cannot be claimed later *unless* you have written evidence of the promise. I am speaking not just for the employer's benefit, but for the employee's, as well. By putting everything in writing, not only does the employer have to pay what is promised, but the employee is crystal clear on what was promised. As I suggested above, feel free to conclude the documentation with "If I don't hear back from you within (24/48/72 hours...), I will assume that you agree to the contents..."

The same applies to project budgeting. It won't help you defend why you overspent by $50,000 with the "CFO's approval," if you have no written documentation of that approval. Please, as soon as you get approval to spend, follow that conversation up in writing.

💬 Story

> A CEO met with the board president to get his feedback on budgeting. In the conversation, he was told that he had approval to spend an additional $250,000 on staff retention. The CEO went on to roll out a plan to offer employees whole life insurance, an insurance policy that is extremely valuable to employees who stay with the company for an extended amount of time. The plan worked like a charm and within six months, 15 employees signed on, thereby almost ensuring long-term commitments to stay with the company. The CEO was thrilled with the results and presented his findings at the next board meeting. After concluding his presentation, one of the board members asked him who granted him the funds to roll

out this project. He pointed to the president who looked slightly puzzled. "We definitely had the conversation, but I don't remember promising that kind of money. I would never have done so without approval from the board. Do you have any back-up?" Without that written documentation, the CEO found himself squirming in his seat for a very long time.

ACCURATE FINANCES

As mentioned earlier, physically tracking revenue and expenses makes a world of difference. This may be obvious to some of you who work at larger companies. If you can remember, think back to the beginning, when as a solopreneur or growing, small-business owner, you had your personal and business accounts intertwined. Putting aside the accounting nightmare, how can you track your company's growth without accurate records? When entrepreneurs tell me their business isn't doing well, and I probe for further information, too often this is what I hear: "Well, each month I can't pay my bills. I have so many tuition expenses, and medical bills." Yes, what you are saying is true. Life is expensive. But that doesn't mean your business isn't healthy. It means that your personal expenses are higher than your business revenue. It doesn't mean your business model is flawed. It means you are ready to grow your business. To be successful, you must list all your revenue and expenses—personal and professional—separately. Open a separate bank account for your personal expenses, and use a separate credit card.

When borrowing money, or reimbursing loans, please document all terms and conditions. What I don't mean is pages and pages that nobody reads. (Leave that for the bank.) Rather, I mean interest terms, how many months till the payback is over, and the refinance option. Although legal documentation is inevitable when borrowing from a bank, small personal loans, with employees laying out money or owing money, can be the source of much heartache.

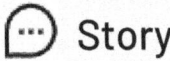 Story

Shari managed a small team at her non-profit. The eight team members had a great relationship, both in and out of the office. They all cared about each other, attended each other's celebrations and never missed a birthday. So, when Stephen asked Shari for a meeting and then shared with her some financial hardships, she wasn't taken aback. Everyone knew that Stephen didn't have an easy life, and he had shared his personal struggles many times with the group. She was surprised, though, that this time, Stephen requested $5,000 to help with car trouble. Of course, Shari wanted to help him, and as it was his first request of the sort, she responded by saying she would do what she could to help. Shari asked her higher-ups and after a few quick meetings, Shari was able to secure the money as a loan that would need to be paid back within 12 months. Shari went back happily to Stephen. Although he was thankful for the email that Shari showed him, explaining the terms, Stephen requested a two-year payback term, instead. After much discussion back and forth, they settled on a loan of $3000 over year one and $2,000 over year two. Stephen happily agreed and said thank you.

Now at this point you might be wondering what the problem is. A plan was finalized. Well, was it? Yes, they knew it was a loan of $3,000 in year one. But could it all have been paid back on the 365th day of year one? Did the managers want to see more progress? Would they get antsy in year one, if none had been paid back during that first year?

Thankfully, in this case, more specific terms were laid out. But imagine how uncomfortable it would have become in the office when 11 months went by without any of the money loaned being paid back.

By now, it goes without saying that the terms and conditions should always be in writing.

This chapter offers plenty of examples of instances when it just makes good sense to document. And in many of these cases, it's essential that what you document be shared with concerned parties. What if those concerned don't agree with your summary of a meeting, or your conclusions about any changes you believe were agreed upon? Documentation is meant to provide firm confidence that you and your partner, or your team, are on the same page going forward. That's why it is critical that you share what you document, and do so promptly, so that everyone is on the same page about the decisions made and the steps going forward.

One final note before we move on, if you are feeling nervous about sharing what you've documented, I recommend that you prepare your partner or team: Before the meeting or call ends, give them a quick heads-up that you will be sending them a brief email or text documenting the outcome of the meeting. Documentation is a key, foundational step in building a strong partnership or team, and so is peace of mind for all concerned.

SCAN ME

RESOURCES:

Download "Essential Clarity Checklists" related to this chapter, including both a Before *You Sign* guide and a *Common Blind Spots* cheat sheet, at

meiraspivak.com/putitinwriting

CHAPTER TWO

Hiring & Firing

In the previous chapter, documentation as it relates to hiring and firing was introduced in more general terms. In this chapter, we begin to dive into this important subject in depth.

As of the printing of this book, the job market continues to be a source of stress for both business owners and potential employees. Although the market is extremely competitive and many individuals seeking jobs find it extremely difficult to find one, there is still a plethora of companies with key positions unfilled. Recruiting bonuses and sign-up incentives have become all the rage, but are they helping get the right people on the bus? Currently, c-suite executives often find themselves underwhelmed by the capabilities and talents of their new hires, and terminations are not infrequent after only a few months. How can we help companies ensure that the chances are good that they will be able to successfully hire and retain new employees?

JOB DESCRIPTION

The first step is the job description. After a quick AI search for a sample job description, here is some of what was suggested.

1. **Position Summary**

    A concise overview of the job's purpose and primary function.

2. **Job Responsibilities**

A detailed list of the tasks and duties the employee will be expected to perform.

Example: "Develop and implement marketing campaigns, manage social-media presence, analyze marketing data, and collaborate with sales teams."

3. **Required Skills and Qualifications**

Specific skills, knowledge and abilities needed to perform the job successfully.

4. **Education and Experience**

Specify the required educational background and years of relevant experience.

5. **Working Conditions**

Describe the work environment and any physical demands of the job.

6. **Reporting Structure**

Indicate who the employee will report to and any supervisory responsibilities.

7. **Other Considerations**

Additional information to consider includes specific software or tools used, certifications required, or any unique aspects of the role.

Seems basic enough, right?

Job Responsibilities

In fact, what we need to focus on is the second qualification on the above list—job responsibilities. To give one example, describing job responsibilities as "develop and implement marketing campaigns, manage social-media presence, analyze marketing data, and collaborate with sales teams," is actually of no help at all. Vague, sweeping statements like these neither direct the employee's time and efforts, nor do they give managers any way of evaluating the employee's work.

Objectives and Key Results (OKRs) were introduced in the discussion of accountability in Chapter One. I expect it's probably obvious why determining objectives and key results is paramount in any discussion of job responsibilities: OKRs ensure that your employees know exactly what they need to do in order to be successful, as well as telling you how to measure their efforts.

OKRs should be knit seamlessly into the job description, because although the description cannot list, or even foresee, every potential project, it *can* list key efforts that an employee will need to make so they understand the type of a job they'll be doing. Many college graduates would apply for a job description to "manage social-media presence," or "develop and implement marketing campaigns." But would they apply for a job where the following is the description:

1. Create 10 social-media posts weekly across four platforms (Instagram, TikTok, LinkedIn and X), hitting 10,000 followers on each platform by the end of the fiscal year.

2. Develop three marketing campaigns monthly for a cross-section of the company.

3. Film and edit a creative video of "employees at work" to send out in a weekly newsletter.

Now whether or not you think these efforts are achievable, listing them as part of a position's responsibilities will do the following:

- It will weed out less qualified applicants.

- It will ensure that expectations are clear. Applicants know what they are getting themselves into and what barometer you use to measure success.

- Later discussions with an employee around growth and promotion will be measured against the job description.

Let's delve further.

Focused job descriptions help weed out less qualified applicants.

In today's job markets, job descriptions are typically posted either by recruiters or on platforms such as Indeed, Glassdoor, LinkedIn and even Craigslist. Applicants submit their resume for hundreds of positions a day, either directly or via bots, often not giving much thought to the positions for which they are applying. This creates a lot of unnecessary work for companies, who need to weed through thousands of job descriptions for each open position. It's true that creating a proper job description won't eliminate AI workarounds, but it *can* greatly reduce the number of submissions. That's because fewer applicants will submit an application for a job where the description is very specific and focused.

A well-defined job description helps ensure clear expectations.

Here's a comment no manager ever wants to hear: "I didn't realize this would be the work." Why? Why didn't your employee realize? How is it possible that they didn't know the type of work that needed to be done? I guess "manage social-media presence" wasn't specific enough.

 **Story**

Ivy league college X hired a recruiter to bring in students from local high schools. The job description included phrases like "attract and recruit talented students," and "build relationships with educational institutions." Bryan was hired for the job immediately, as he was extremely personable and loved offering guidance to students. What made him the perfect candidate was that he was a recent graduate of one of the local high schools. Bryan's first few weeks on the job went all right, as Bryan spent the time visiting his alma matter and surrounding schools and building relationships. After about a month, his manager sat down with him to review his progress.

"I've made great connections," Bryan assured his boss. "I've spoken to a dozen teachers and countless students."

"Amazing," was the reply. "And how many students have come in for a tour?"

"What do you mean?" Bryan asked.

"How many students have toured the school? How many parents have you called this week? How many seniors have you grabbed coffee with?"

"Oh..."

When the conversation started to falter, Bryan's manager got to the bottom of things. "What's really going on here, Bryan? Do you like the job?"

"Yes, I love it," Bryan assured his boss. "I love making relationships and guiding people."

"Amazing. Do you know what you were hired to do?"

"Yes," Bryan answered confidently. "Answer students' questions about the school so more students come here."

"Well, not exactly. You weren't hired to respond to

student and parent inquiries. You were hired to recruit students. That entails going out of your way to start conversations, cold-calling parents and students, as well as giving as many tours as possible. Did you know that?"

"Um...yes, I guess?"

"Well, let me ask you. Do you like recruiting? Do you want to be reaching out to people all day?"

"Not really," admits Bryan."

"But you know this is a recruiting job, right?"

"Yes."

"Do you want to stay in this job?"

"I think so..."

"You're a great guy, but it's clear this position isn't within your comfort zone. How about we sit down to brainstorm what might be a better fit?"

"I'd love that."

Although the manager did a great job making Bryan feel safe enough to admit that he was in the wrong role, this entire scenario could have been avoided with clearer expectations. Instead of the job description listing "attract and recruit talented students" it could have said "call 50 potential families weekly" or "meet with five high school seniors weekly for at least 30 minutes each." More specific descriptions are a bit intimidating, but they definitely would have set the stage for clearer expectations—*before* Bryan was hired.

> Later discussions around growth and promotion will be measured against the job description.

It's annual review time. Although some businesses might do a good job at these, I think it is safe to say that most of them can be improved. Currently what's typical is for a manager to start by predetermining an employee's raise (or lack thereof), and then sitting down together with his direct report and pretending that the review actually means anything at all. He will jot down notes and even send a post-meeting summary. He will use buzzwords like aligned, collaborative and innovative, and will even give the employee direct feedback on the spot. It will feel nice and the manager will have checked all the HR boxes. The only problem is that the engagement is meaningless.

Here's what *should* happen instead. The meeting should feel natural, as the manager already meets weekly with his direct report to review challenges and offer support. Thus, the employee knows where he stands going into the meeting, and there should be no major surprises. During the official review time, the manager should take out the job description and review the employee's progress towards fulfilling the description. If the employee is "crushing it," it should be obvious, and raises, bonuses and promotions should be directly tied to the success of his efforts. The meeting will conclude with a follow-up in writing and next steps.

FIRING

Unfortunately, terminations are inevitable as companies grow. Employees underperform, or don't even perform at all. Some are lazy and some are negligent. Some have a poor work ethic, and some are dishonest. Whatever the case, in order to avoid a lawsuit, and to satisfy HR, here are the key steps to ensuring that you've crossed all your t's and dotted all your i's, once it is clear that terminating a staff person's employment is necessary.

Be sure there is a paper trail.

Putting things in writing has never been more important than when it comes to firing. All you need is for a terminated employee to accuse you of mistreatment, abuse or misconduct for you to face a lifetime of misery. If your only defense in the face of accusations is a few anecdotes of times showing he showed up late to the office, you're going to need a very expensive lawyer. Here are the steps to proper documentation.

1. As soon as you start noticing a trend, have a conversation with the staff member about his undesirable behavior. Tell him what you've been noticing and set up a new plan for success. Tell him that you will be sending a follow-up email for documentation purposes, and that he should look it over and reply back within X hours if anything is incorrect. In the email, document all the instances when the employee acted inappropriately. At the bottom of the follow-up email, conclude with "If I don't hear back from you within

(24/48/72 hours...), I will assume that you agree to the contents of this email."

2. Repeat Step 1 two to three times, as needed. Loop in HR with updates.

3. If the issue persists or is getting worse, have another in-person conversation. This time say that you've tried to help, and you need to see improvement. Lack of improvement will lead to consequences, and possibly termination. Follow up the conversation with an email in writing.

4. Once enough documentation is gathered, termination is appropriate.

An important note: When a serious infraction occurs, then it may be that fewer steps, or even no steps at all, are needed. In some cases, an employee should be terminated immediately. In those situations, you should not wait for further infringements before termination, as their presence at the company is jeopardizing the emotional and/or physical wellbeing of other employees. HR should be consulted as the process escalates.

💬 Story

> Laura was always coming late to work and skipping team meetings. She was extremely disorganized, and dealing with family challenges meant she started off

her mornings on the wrong foot. Laura always mumbled an apology as she walked in, but her tardiness was starting to impact the office. Other staff were coming late to work, and meetings were starting consistently late while they waited for her to arrive. Laura's manager wanted to approach her, but kept looking the other way, hoping her bad behavior would just disappear. Then one Wednesday, a major presentation was planned for 9 a.m. the next day. Laura was reminded to arrive on time, as the president of a client bank was going to be in attendance. Despite the importance of the meeting, Laura showed up at 9:20 a.m. and fumbled for her seat. The bank's president looked up, surprised by the unprofessionalism of the team. Laura's company ended up losing the account; Laura's manager spent the day stewing. She finally approached Laura, told her that she was fuming and that she didn't think it was working out for Laura to stay with the company.

"What do you mean?" asked Laura. "What are you talking about? You never spoke to me about this issue in a serious way. How was I supposed to know it was very important. I always assumed if you cared, you would have said something. I'm sorry about what happened today. My son threw up this morning and it was out of my control. I'll try to be better in the future." Upset at herself, the manager walked out of the office, realizing that she had never created a paper trail. For now, they were stuck with Laura. But at least the manager was going to learn from her mistakes: She went back to her office and sent Laura a stern email documenting what happened, and reiterating the importance of coming on time. "Well, I've learned my lesson. I hope Laura learns hers, too."

WORKING CONDITIONS

Another aspect of a job to document clearly is the workspace itself. It's fifth in the list suggested by our AI search for the components of a job description.

Working conditions describe the work environment and any physical demands of the job. It is crucial that your job description state what type of work is necessary. Must the job applicant have a license in order to pick up and deliver orders, or be in good enough physical condition to handle packages? Will there be heavy packages to handle, exceeding, say, 30 pounds? If so, those conditions of employment must be stated clearly to avoid issues later. Included in this might be exposure to different temperatures—indoors or out—and the ability to work in a noisy environment. The last thing you want later is for an employee to perform poorly because of previous neck or back injuries, or because they can only concentrate when it's quiet. The more you document in advance, the safer you are.

Be sure to include in your job description the things that no one wants to talk about—annoying jobs like straightening up the break room or locking up at night. Although we might be afraid a prospective applicant will lose interest as a result, if you don't include those responsibilities, it will likely backfire later. If someone needs to open up the office or facility in the morning, they must know this is part of their job, and realize that if they arrive late to work, the entire office will be held up.

CONTRACTS

Contracts, or terms and conditions, can prove to be very useful should things go wrong. Thinking about possible scenarios will help avoid future discrepancies.

 Story

Camp R hired multiple teenagers to serve as staff. Some were paid a salary of, let's say, $1,000, while the compensation for others included a package of salary plus tips. (That would total $500 plus an estimated $250.) Although anyone on a camp's staff can be challenging, asking teenaged staff, in particular, to maintain a level of responsibility they aren't used to can cause a number of problems, to put it mildly. One particular staff member at the camp needed to be sent home after just two of the four weeks of camp, as she had clearly violated a camp rule. It was no longer safe for her to remain in camp, and she was sent home at the parents' expense. About two weeks after the camp session ended, the camp director received a call from the mother of the staffer who had been sent home. In addition to blaming the director for her daughter's behavior, she also demanded compensation for the two out of the four weeks her daughter had worked—a total of $500. "Why should my daughter not be compensated for the time she served on staff!" demanded the mother. After about 30 minutes of back and forth, the camp director ran out of steam, eventually agreeing to compensation of $500. Frustrated, the director resolved to address this problem for the coming year.

He had learned his lesson. The next year, upon the completion of staff training, every staff member signed a contract restating the camp rules and confirming that if they were caught violating any of those rules, they accepted that they would be terminated and entitled to zero salary and/or tips.

The following year, a similar challenge occurred. One of the teenagers was incapable of doing his job. He was lazy and had limited executive functioning skills. The director often found the counselor sleeping on a bench in the gym instead of leading a basketball game and watching over his campers. This counselor had been told at the beginning of the summer that he would receive a salary of $250 plus tips. (As before, tips would average about another $250.) Since the teen did a terrible job with the children, the director wanted to give him only $100 in collected tips. But after consulting with others, he ended up paying the teen the full amount—both to prevent future problems and to avoid dealing with the teenager's parent. For the next year, the director changed the policy so that tips would now be "performance-based." This is written clearly in the job-acceptance email and allows the director to use his own discretion when making these financial decisions.

TERMINATING—AND BEGINNING—PARTNERSHIPS

Now let's consider partnerships, starting with how they commonly begin. When a business partnership is formed, it is often between two friends or individuals with mutual respect and a shared idea for a business. Feeling euphoric, they get started, excited about the road ahead. In a perfect scenario, the relationship is intact until the end, and their business continues to flourish. But in certain scenarios, it doesn't go smoothly, and cracks begin to erode the foundation. Here are several, common reasons that partnerships might dissolve:

- Financial disagreements
- Fundamental business disagreements
- Personal issues
- Breach of contract

If problems arise for these or any other reason, tension begins to rise, and friendships can quickly dissolve. This is why forethought is vital. Before entering into a partnership, key issues need to be addressed and documented "just in case." Here, the use of a lawyer might make sense. And even though the discussion may be premature, and can be very uncomfortable, having the conversation can make a world of a difference going forward. Some areas of your business you might want to have documented include:

- What is the profit-sharing arrangement for your partnership, now and if one partner exits?

- Does a non-compete clause need to be drafted?

- How are disputes settled?

- What happens with shared clients down the line? Private clients now?

Again, being uncomfortable now can make a world of difference later.

💬 Story

Marley and Jim had become business partners many years before. They had never written anything up formally, because "that's just not how it was done back then." After all, they were friends, and friends don't get into these fights. Fast forward 30 years, and Marley is thinking of retiring and having her son Ben take over. Well, Jim doesn't exactly love Ben, who is a millennial and often comes across as feeling entitled. He likes

Ben's work but would rather not work with him. Jim feels backed into a corner with no alternative. He tells Marley that if she retires, he'd like to continue on his own. Marley is upset, as she didn't work all these years for it all to go down the drain. Well, fighting ensued, and eventually Jim left and sold his share to Ben (at a 35% profit share). In the end, no one was happy and their friendship was never the same. The one thing everyone agreed on was that they wished they had documented everything long before.

EXIT INTERVIEWS

It is not uncommon for organizations to hold exit interviews before an employee leaves. Although they can take place after someone is terminated, they most commonly happen when employees leave at will. They may be moving locations or have taken a job elsewhere that pays better. Exit interviews are normally held during an employee's last week of work, perhaps on their last day. The idea is to gather feedback while the employee's feelings and thoughts are still fresh. Documenting these interviews can be helpful in finding trends and patterns. If, for example, 80% of people leave due to lack of growth opportunities, then the company can use that data to reexamine its current trajectory. If they leave due to poor managers, then the company can offer better training programs. Evaluating information gathered over time can give the company a richer, fuller perspective.

SCAN ME

RESOURCE:

For specialized tools that support non-profit agreements, freelance contracts and event documentation, download the "Professional Agreements Toolkit" at

meiraspivak.com/putitinwriting

CHAPTER THREE

Documentation for Effective Leadership

This chapter turns to more focused aspects of documentation that are vital for healthy company leadership, though much of the advice offered here would be equally helpful to any one of us.

POLICY EXCEPTIONS

If policies exist in your business, so do policy exceptions. Those should be documented, too. If you own a large jewelry shop, and extend a 10% discount to employees, and a 20% discount to family, that needs to be documented. Creating clear policies now means fewer problems later. And, of course, sticking to those policies is key.

 Story

> Trevor ran the local construction company; everyone in town used him, as his was the only show. Trevor loved supporting local events and tried to sponsor them when he could. One day, his nephew called and asked if Trevor would sponsor his local little league team. The price tag was $2,500. Although Trevor normally spent only $1,500 to sponsor this type of event, he made a one-time exception for his adorable

nephew. About two weeks later, the calls started coming in from elsewhere for more sponsorships, now asking for more than he had previously been donating. Non-profits in the area had noticed that Trevor had upped his game and were now seeking a piece of the pie. Because Trevor had made an exception for his nephew, rather than adhering to his policy of restricting donation requests to friends and family, he found himself in a pickle. He ended up donating more than he wanted to. After that, he went back to the old drawing board and reconsidered the way he wanted to donate, and created more lasting policies that would help him remain consistent going forward.

DECISION-MAKING FOR LIFE

There are a number of times in life when we come to a crossroads and face life-altering decisions. These can include choosing a college, committing to a spouse, and selecting schools for your kids. These decisions are more pivotal, as their impact can truly alter your life's course. The college you attend and the friends and educators you surround yourself with can greatly impact who you are as a person. The person you marry can greatly impact the person you become, as well as the way you contribute to the world. Coming full circle, the friends and educators you choose for your children can greatly impact their lives. The same would apply to walking away from a marriage, a business partnership or even a relationship with a close friend. These decisions can have vast repercussions. When it comes to making these pivotal types of decisions, you should devote a significant amount of time to doing so.

Making a list of pros and cons is key. It is not enough to just *feel* a pull towards or away from a business relationship—or school or spouse—we also need to *know* what the right thing is. Distractions are not useful when you are trying to make a potentially life-altering decision about your business. Focusing on listing your thoughts and feelings, and deciding whether each is a pro or a con, not only helps you think through all the options, it forces you to stare at yourself in the face. It might not seem like a big deal that your friends are up till 10 p.m. every night pursuing their side hustles, but you may have a spouse and children at home who need you there in the evening. The fact that the man you are considering going into partnership with doesn't always treat you with respect can be brushed off with excuses—he was tired or he had a bad day—but when you document the fact that "he doesn't always treat me with respect," it should help you decide if this is a the right business partner for you.

Instead of a traditional list of pros and cons, I'd add a few steps.

- **Step 1 –** Pull out a fresh piece of paper or create a new Google document for yourself. At the top, clearly state the decision you need to make and the goal in making the decision. Perhaps the decision is whether to accept a new job opportunity, and the goal might be:

    Example: To find a work situation that aligns with my values.

Example: To work a three-day work week so I can prioritize my family.

- **Step 2** – Underneath the decision and the goal, write this question: Should I take this position?

- **Step 3** – Draw up your list of pros and cons.

- **Step 4** – Assign a weight to each pro and con based on its impact:

    1 = Low impact
    2 = Medium impact
    3 = High impact

- **Step 5** – Review the lists in light of your goal. If the answer still is not clear, add up the numbers in each column. The column with the ***higher total*** has more impact and should carry more weight in your decision.

Here's an example:

- **Step 1** – Write the goal: To work a three-day work week and prioritize my family.

- **Step 2** – Write the question: Should I take the job at the law firm?

- **Step 3** – Make your lists:

    Pros:

    - Great salary
    - Great people
    - Includes lunch

    Cons:

    - Often have to stay late
    - Often have to work weekends
    - Far from your home

- **Step 4** – Order the list:

    Pros:

    - Great salary – 3
    - Great people – 2
    - Includes Lunch – 1

    Cons:

    - Often have to stay late – 3
    - Often have to work weekends – 3
    - Far from your home – 3

- **Step 5** – Analyze the pros and cons as compared to your goal.

    - Your conclusion: The cons outweigh the pros 9:6.
    - This is not the job opportunity you should pursue.

INDECISIVENESS

If you tend to be indecisive, the activity I just described will prove to be a challenge for you. You will look at this list, and possibly fixate on just one or two of the positives, allowing them to distract you from making a rational decision based on the total picture your lists provide. To you I say, trust the process! If you naturally make more feeling-based decisions, and you know that has caused you harm in the past, this system will protect you from that tendency.

In business, it is important to document your decision-making trail, so that later, when you look back, you can see why you made those decisions. Why did you choose one vendor or one pricing structure over another? It can be so very frustrating to find yourself repeating the same conversations—with yourself or perhaps with your business partner or spouse—when a quick glance at your list can give you the insight you need. Providing a decision paper trail also helps you avoid finger-pointing later when someone in a meeting asks, "Who decided this, anyway?"

SCHEDULING AND CALENDARING

I don't imagine this book will become a *New York Times* bestseller just because I am recommending that you physically input your appointments and events into a calendar. But it is important! Yes, we all know that the times when we mess up our appointments are either when we don't write them down, or we write them down incorrectly. Here are a few tips to ensure we don't forget to take care of this crucial bit of daily housekeeping.

- As soon as you make an appointment, add it to your calendar. I recommend a phone calendar, or any other calendar *provided it always comes with you.* It is extremely unhelpful to use a paper calendar that sits on your desk when you are at a networking event trying to schedule meetings. It's challenging to try to make them on the phone. And once you hang up, the odds increase exponentially that you will later forget to add it to your calendar. This is not due to negligence, but rather to the fact that you can be easily interrupted.

- When adding the appointment, include all relevant information: the address (including the floor/room number), and the phone number, in case you later need it.

- If the appointment isn't confirmed, put it in as tentative until it is. But do not hold the space for more than a few days, unless it is a crucial appointment.

- Having access to your spouse and children's calendars can be very helpful in avoiding conflicts.

- When you know your work schedule, or spouse and/or children's school calendars, add in their important dates (conferences, days off, in-school events, and so on), so that you don't double-book.

- If you cannot write down an appointment right away—don't have your calendar, don't have time—at a minimum set an alarm to remind yourself to record it later. Keep snoozing or rescheduling the alarm until you've taken care of adding it. Do not skip this step!

CLARIFYING THOUGHTS AND FEELINGS

In truth, when you are facing *any* important decision, writing can be an effective tool in gaining clarity and self-knowledge. We are all bombarded with noise throughout the day, in both a physical and metaphysical sense. We are constantly busy, our minds racing to keep up with our latest to-do list. Our phones ding and buzz and ring off the hook, making it hard to stay present. As a result, it's no surprise that journaling has become more popular, not just as a way to record what's happening in your life, but also as a way to clear your head of all that noise, and process your thoughts and feelings.

Journaling might come naturally for some, but for others it's a struggle. Here are some tips on how to use journals to help clarify your own feelings:

1. Try to journal daily. The more you journal, the better your journal. (It's really true!)

2. Sitting down to a blank page can be daunting. Instead, try starting every session with a prompt or a topic to help guide your brain about what to think about. "The people at work." "Should I continue to date her?" "How am I doing financially?" Prompts like these give you a topic without taking away your freedom of expression. They provide a closed world for your brain to know what to write about. I will share more about the concept of the closed world in Chapter Six.

3. Then, focus on a two-part process:

- **PART A:** Wrestle with your thoughts. Why are you upset with a colleague? Did he really do something wrong or are you jealous of his promotion? Why do you keep losing it at home? Is it really because you had a hard day at work or do you just take out your aggression on the people you love most? Why are you so afraid of taking a medication? When did you first develop the stigma about it?

- **PART B:** Rewrite your story.

One two-part question that can be helpful in directing you towards root causes is this: "When's the earliest memory you have of feeling this way? When you think of this memory, what story did you tell yourself in that moment that has continued to impact your life?"

💬 Story

Sam has struggled with sitting still since he was a child. Now 42, he is trying to get to the root of the problem, as it's having a negative impact. He can't sit through boring meetings, is constantly fidgeting in his seat and especially hates filling out paperwork. Although his job mostly involves hands-on projects, where he does stay on task, he has gotten into trouble by not paying bills and not filling out his paternity time-off forms in a timely way, causing him significant financial loss. When the topic of ADHD medication arises, Sam replies that he really doesn't want to take any medication for it. He had taken it once as a child and he has a negative association with it.

The backstory: When Sam was 10 years old, one of his teachers was at his wit's end trying to deal with Sam. After many conversations with Sam's parents about the difficulty their son was having staying still, medication had been prescribed and started. Sam had always been embarrassed about taking it and didn't tell his friends about it, as few kids were taking them. One day, when he was misbehaving in class, his teacher announced: "Sam, what is wrong with you? Why can't you sit still? Did you forget to take your meds today?" Sam melted in his chair and wasn't sure which he was feeling more—embarrassment or anger. At that moment, Sam made a choice and told himself that the price of taking medicine wasn't worth it and he would never take ADHD medicine again. This story remained with him until adulthood, where he was still suffering. Sam needed to retry medication but had a mental block because of an incident from his youth. Was 10-year-old Sam correct in declaring that taking meds wasn't worth it? Perhaps. But it certainly wasn't helpful.

Side note: This would fall under the category of TBU, True but Useless, a concept I read about in *New York Times* bestseller *Switch: How to Change Things When*

> *Change Is Hard*, by Chip and Dan Heath.[4] Even if it is true that Sam's teacher's behavior was inappropriate, it would have been useless and unhelpful for Sam to continue with that behavior.
>
> Now much older, Sam takes the time to write down his thoughts about what happened so many years before, and realizes that because of one poorly trained schoolteacher, he had allowed himself to lead a lower quality of life. He realizes it's time to rewrite his story. Instead of saying "I don't take meds because of a negative childhood experience," he says, "I'm open to trying medications because I know they will help me."

The truth is we *all* have a choice about the stories we tell ourselves.

Instead of telling yourself "I'm terrible at sales," say "I won't give up when trying to make a sale, even when it's hard."

Instead of telling yourself "I'm always late to work because my kids are disorganized," say "I have a hard time naturally with time management, so I make systems to keep me on track."

Instead of saying "I can't," when they give me busy work, say "I'm committed to doing a lower-level job for my first year in order to build up my resume."

---

[4] Chip Heath and Dan Heath, *Switch: How to Change Things When Change Is Hard*, Crown Currency, 2010. ISBN-13 978-0935721997.

Instead of saying "I'm so bad at posting on LinkedIn," say "Posting on LinkedIn isn't natural for me, so I will post weekly. Even better, I will post monthly and schedule my weekly posts to go out at one time."

The stories we tell ourselves create our future. Spend time rewriting those stories through journaling.

ALLOWING OTHERS TO HELP

Now this may seem like an odd topic, but unfortunately it must be discussed. There are many capable people in this world who are amazing multitaskers—the do-ers. They can get a lot done at one time, but probably don't do each thing perfectly. The do-ers are extremely capable, and even though they make mistakes, they are an overall asset to their team. They keep everything in their head, and since they always seem busy, you mostly leave them to their own devices. Everything is mostly okay most of the time.

And then one day everything changes. The office gets busier. Everyone is assigned additional projects. You notice that the office do-er, Jane, is overwhelmed and starting to drop balls. She says everything is okay, yet keeps messing up in one capacity or another. She says she doesn't need help, but you see the bigger picture. You ask Jane for a meeting to see how you and others can best assist, but she honestly doesn't know. "Just help, I guess," she mumbles unhelpfully. "You can follow me around and work with me if you want." Well, that's not exactly what you meant...

For employees like Jane, it is extremely important that they keep a physical list of tasks they need to accomplish. This way, not only can they check off the box as they've accomplished a task, but others can help them by seeing what jobs are left. Of course, this is easier said than done, because people like Jane don't always have the patience to make the list in the first place. If you are the manager supervising someone like Jane, take the time at the beginning of every project to sit with them and develop the list. Over time, list-making will become more natural, and often lists for past projects can be duplicated to get Jane started on a new project. But having Jane write out the list is a crucial first step.

COMPANY CULTURE

Company culture refers to a shared set of beliefs, values and attitudes. It's the way people feel when they are at your company, when they interact with your staff, when they engage with your product. When company culture is done right, it can shape the overall work environment, impacting the experience of both employees and customers. Culture is not just something nice to have. It's a necessity.

People often mistakenly think of company culture as a trend or theme that disappears when an event Is over. Company culture should withstand the passage of time and trying situations. It shouldn't include employees playing favorites with one client. It should be a standard that applies throughout your company.

If your office has a culture of being fun and innovative, that should be reflected in how employees answer the phone and in the office décor. If you showed up, and the office furniture looked like it was from 1980, you wouldn't get the fun and innovative vibe. It doesn't mean you need to switch furniture every year, nor do you need to crack jokes all day, but the overall feeling should be one of fun. If your team has a culture of "customers first," then employees should be encouraged to give up their lunch break to serve clients. (I hope you can see why some company cultures can become problematic!) If the culture is "the customer is always right," then you need to be prepared to both give a lot of refunds *and* make sure your product is so amazing that no one ever complains.

It is vital that you write down a statement about your company's culture. Doing so calls for clarity. With clarity comes understanding by all employees and a sense of unity. And when you hang that statement on your office wall, it calls for extreme accountability. Are you really committed to excellence? Then why did you cut the recent upgrade on your software? Do you really foster a culture of growth? Then why did you cancel your professional development conference? Do you really have a culture of philanthropy? Then why don't you match your employees' donations? Reading the writing on the wall ensures follow-through on your company's culture.

Additionally, writing down the culture statement, or even an "about us" statement, allows for potential new employees to see, before applying, if the company would be a good fit. If the application states that "we believe that trees are as important as people," then it will weed out non-environmentalists. If it states that "we value in-person work with clients," then it will weed out applicants looking to work remotely. And if it says that "we emphasize a culture of open communication and collaboration," then it will weed out introverts who prefer to work independently.

In addition to policies about the culture of your company, documenting your stance on vendor selection, diversity and inclusion, as well as environmental commitments, can protect your reputation if questions arise later. Other, less obvious policies that may be relevant for your organization are beyond the scope of this book.

EXIT PLANNING AND SUCCESSION

As we age, we begin to think about planning for our family's future. How will they manage? How will we manage? Have we set ourselves and our families up financially? Can we afford care if we need it, so we don't become a financial burden? We write wills to legally document these plans and avoid arguments or disagreements between loved ones. We also want to ensure that funds are left for the charities that we feel most need it.

Well, the same must be true for our businesses. What is your ultimate desire for your business's future? Would you like a child to take over when you retire, or do you plan to sell or exit? Do you want to keep the business in the family or give it up entirely? What will your role be? If you sell, will you still work for the new owner or will you spend most of your day golfing, volunteering or traveling? You don't need to know the answers to these questions now, but here are three key directives.

1. **Make yourself replaceable.**

    Replaceable? Yes!!! Replaceable. If you are the only person in your company who you can handle a certain task, you are taking a tremendous risk, often referred to as a "key man risk." It always irks me when I need something done by a team and the response is "sorry, X is on maternity leave, and she's the only one who knows how to do it." That is literally crazy. Let's say X leaves, or passes on. Will the company just stop performing that essential task? If you are the only one who knows your company's secret sauce, then the company lives and dies by you. You *MUST* ensure that a few people understand how to do each job, and that they know how to train others. This chain of command must be written down.

Example: **Filling out form X:**

- First in command – Tonya
- Next – Bruce
- Third – Shona

Shona is capable of training new people.

Example: **Demonstrating X product:**

- Best salesman – Sam
- Next – Dahlia
- Third – Jack

Sam trains one new employee each month, and reviews with them quarterly.

This doesn't mean that every employee needs to know how to do everything, but *NOTHING* should live and die with you. Write down everything you know how to do, and ensure that others can do it, too, even if they cannot perform at your level.

Note: The concept "key man risk" describes just this vulnerability: it describes a business whose success depends on one or a few individuals.

2. **Write down your goal.**

   For most business owners it should be "I want to create a sellable business." Then work backwards to hit that goal. For your business to be sellable, you determine that it must be at X level of income, have Y number of recurring revenue and Z level of scalable programs. Keep that goal hanging on your wall, and remember it every single day.

3. **Don't assume anyone will know what you are thinking.**

   Legal documentation must be written down to ensure that there is no funny business later. The last thing your company needs after your passing is for a partner to announce that you told everyone that he would become the full owner for a low price, when *you* had planned for your son to continue the family business. No documentation means no insurance that your desires will be implemented. Nobody reads minds, and your thoughts, your intentions, will remain just that.

Additionally, many people write ethical wills, a document where they share their values and the legacy they want to leave behind. Traditionally, it is done for loved ones but can also be done for a business. Note, that an ethical will is not binding, and will not hold up in court, but it can serve as a north star for those trying to live out your mission. A business ethical will is a beautiful complement to a legal will, as it provides context and guidance as a legacy for a business. An ethical will for loved ones might include a hope for them to follow a certain religious path, remain close to family members and continue to share similar values, while an ethical will for a business might convey the owner's values, lessons learned through hardship and future aspirations.

CHAPTER FOUR

What *NOT* to Put in Writing

Finally, the truth comes out! I was serious that you really *shouldn't* actually put everything in writing. I'm sure you can think of times in your life when you sent an email or text and deeply regretted it later. Perhaps it was a last word of revenge you sent to a spouse, a business partner or employee. Maybe it was a discount that you wish you had never offered. Or perhaps it was a resignation letter that by next morning you regretted sending. In short, don't commit to writing anything you'll regret later.

Unlike verbal conversations, written correspondence has an obvious, added dimension that adds to its severity: It can be very hard to retract. In some situations, it's impossible to retract. Worst case scenario, the words in your email or post could be forwarded to millions of people in a matter of seconds, causing irreparable pain. And no amount of regret you feel afterwards will help the situation, nor will it allow for an undo. The words you should never have used, never have said, have entered the worldwide web, where they could be recalled later by almost anyone. With those cautionary words in mind, here are four guiding principles for knowing when not to put something in writing:

1. When it's something you might later regret writing

2. When it's something that can be taken out of context and forwarded

3. When it's something you don't want recorded for posterity

4. When it should really be a conversation and you were avoiding discomfort

GUIDING PRINCIPLE #1: WHEN IT'S SOMETHING YOU MIGHT LATER REGRET WRITING

 Story

You've been working hard on a building project over the last few weeks. In fact, you've been consistently staying till 10 p.m. most nights—all the leaders are. Well, except for one person. Your team consists of Brian, Lea, Ed and yourself and although most of you are really pulling your weight, Ed is definitely not. He leaves every day promptly at 5:00 p.m., priding himself on his work-life balance. He picks up one of his kids at day care and can't be later than 5:15 p.m. You accept this halfheartedly, not understanding why his wife can't pick up his child from day care. After all, you also have three kids are home. This is crunch time for the building project. The entire team is needed this week and then by Sunday it will all be over. The hardest part about this situation is that Ed is a childhood friend, and, honestly, he's acted like this for years. You shouldn't have expected more. You mutter under your breath but can't really take it any more when he walks out the door on Thursday night at 5 p.m. You shoot him a text:

"Ed, this is not okay. Cut the garbage and get a babysitter. I know you've been doing this your whole life but this time you are really letting down the whole team. Shape up, or give up your seat for someone else."

You press send, not wanting to think of the ramifications of *not* sending it. Almost instantaneously you feel bad. This is one of your longest-standing friendships. How could you do this to him?

You keep checking your phone. No response. Did he get the text? Is he mad? Should you call him to apologize even though you're really mad at *him*? After two hours of waiting, you decide to call. No answer. You try back an hour later. No answer. At about midnight you text him again.

"Sorry man. I apologize. I was just upset. I hope you forgive me."

No response. You barely sleep that night, tossing and turning with regret. When you get to the office the next day, Ed isn't there. That's weird, you think. Ed always arrives first. When you don't see him all day, you call his wife, Barbara. She answers. She's actually worried as well, and she mentions that she doesn't know what happened, but since last night, Ed, who has previously struggled with depression, has regressed. He's been in bed all day and she's not sure what to do. You're not either, but you know one thing: you've never in your life regretted a text more.

When you send texts and emails out of anger, sadness, rage or any on a list of myriad, negative feelings, there can rarely be anything good that comes from sending it. Before sending one, ask yourself:

- Will I regret this later?
- Will I even regret just *some* of this later?
- Will I regret even a *tiny* part of this later?

If you answered yes to any of the above questions, don't send the message.

Story

You just had an extremely uncomfortable interaction with an employee. You have spent a lot of money making the office a comfortable place to work, primarily by providing a lot of snacks and drinks. Everyone appreciates it and often grabs two or three snacks a day. For the last few days though, you've noticed that Evan is taking candy and putting it in his backpack to take home. You bought these snacks for use during the day, and not to lower their food bills. You feel uncomfortable approaching him, as it's awkward to have the conversation, so you decide to send an email instead. If you're already thinking you shouldn't email Evan, you're right.

GUIDING PRINCIPLE #2: WHEN IT'S SOMETHING THAT CAN BE TAKEN OUT OF CONTEXT AND SHARED

Whenever you send a text, email or other kind of written communication, you always run the risk of having your message tampered with and/or forwarded to others. With the advent of AI and many editing programs, not only can messages be altered, they can look almost perfectly authentic. You always run a risk in sending a message, even when you try to do so as safely as possible. But it isn't helpful to live in a state of paranoia, so what should you do? Here are four ideas to prevent your messages from being misconstrued.

- **Copy, or blind-copy, others.** When appropriate, include others in the email chain. This way, more people can attest to what was originally written. The same would hold true for group-texting and WhatsApp. The more people who were included initially, the safer you are.

- **Send yourself a copy** (cc yourself) for an additional record.

- **Take a photo of the email/text** with your camera and upload it to Google drive or another program that records the exact time of upload. This way, if someone tampers with it later, you can prove the actual send time.

- **Disable automatic forwarding and utilize encryption and confidentiality settings** when available.

(**Author's note:** I have never used these options.)

GUIDING PRINCIPLE #3: WHEN IT'S SOMETHING YOU DON'T WANT RECORDED FOR POSTERITY

As the spread of technology continues to accelerate, one wrong post and a person's life can be altered negatively. Anything that is written and sent online can potentially be recorded forever. A person should be extremely careful about not only what they look like in pictures, but also the content they produce. One wrong political post can come back to haunt them decades later when they are looking to get involved in politics and their personal history is researched. The same applies to posts with illicit, racial or derogatory content. Always consider first: Do I want this content to be remembered when I am trying to _____? Fill in the blank—get a job, find a spouse, run for office. Better yet, don't sent illicit, racial of derogatory content to begin with!

GUIDING PRINCIPLE #4: WHEN IT SHOULD REALLY BE A CONVERSATION AND YOU WERE AVOIDING DISCOMFORT

We have now reached the most important and prevalent issue. Many of us are afraid of confrontation and try to avoid it at any cost. That fear of confrontation dictates our behavior, and avoidance becomes the name of the game. Rather than having a straightforward conversation with an employee, we send an email. Rather than talk out an issue with a spouse, we play passive-aggressive and hope the issue or feeling miraculously disappears. Rather than speaking to a sibling directly about what to do with a parent's estate, we'll talk negatively about that sibling with every other family member. Avoidance, although easier, is often a grave mistake that leads to more problems after.

Giving direct feedback is a manager's key responsibility. Managers must be aware of their employees' performance so that they can encourage and reinforce positive behavior. They also must notice problems and offer steps for improvement. Weekly meetings, when run properly, ensure constant communication and relationship-building. The time together builds trust and allows employees to let down their guard, increasing openness to growth and feedback for both of you. Despite all this, when proper channels are not in place, managers will still avoid giving proper feedback when they can. They will send an email or even avoid giving feedback altogether. They think they are being kind. In reality, they are hurting their employee's chance for longevity in the company. Here's an example.

> **SUBJECT LINE:** Snacks in the Office
>
> Dear Evan,
>
> It was nice seeing you today, even for just a minute. I wanted to reach out about the snacks in the office. I buy them for office use, but I've noticed that you've been taking them home in your backpack. On Monday, you took a Hershey bar, pretzels and pita chips. On Tuesday, it was three Gatorades, and on Wednesday it was Oreos, peanuts and two waters. We can't have that behavior continue. Please stop it at once.
>
> Looking forward to seeing an improvement.
> Thanks.

Now, at first glance you think to yourself "That seems pretty good to me. It was polite and to the point. Nothing mean, no cursing. What could be wrong?"

Well, the next day when you arrive at the office, one of the following two scenarios occurs.

Scenario 1: You notice people whispering around you and after approaching someone to ask if something is the matter, they mutter that they can't believe you don't trust your employees. How do you expect anyone to want to work here? Plus, do you have so little to do with your time that you notice how many Oreos people take each day? It really is pathetic.

You feel your cheeks get warm with embarrassment, and you rush to your office for a cold drink. You can't believe he shared your email with others! But why? Honestly, you should have known better. Of course, he would use it against you. And since he has the email in writing, there's no way for you to wiggle your way out of it. You're regretting even showing up today.

Scenario 2: You arrive at your office and sit down at your desk to check your emails. You notice one from the director of HR and are shocked when you are asked to attend a meeting about last night's email. When you arrive, the director asks you to describe the situation, which you do. She then asks you if you spoke about the issue with Evan before sending the more formal email? She asks why you chose to respond in writing, and you share that it was more comfortable. You then receive a strong reprimand with an explanation that a formal email should never be the first step.

In either of these two scenarios, it is clear that a verbal conversation should have been the first step. That would have enabled the following three things to happen.

- You could have developed a rapport with Evan, so that he knew that you were on his side.

- You could have nonchalantly started speaking about the snacks and left room for Evan to admit his mistake before you had to reprimand him. You also could have shown empathy and possibly offered a solution in case Evan mentioned any struggles at home.

- In the event that he didn't mention anything, you could have brought up the conversation in the most gentle of tones, all the while being direct.

At the end of that conversation, share that you will send a follow-up in writing to ensure that you are both on the same page. It is then, and only then, that you should send something in writing.

 **Story**

Leslie has been overly domineering during staff meetings. You encourage participation and love that Leslie does so, but often it is too much. She barks at anyone who disagrees with her, and is verbally upset if the group doesn't go with her suggestions. Only six people are in these meetings, and most of them are pushovers. Yes, you notice that Simon, for instance, has really stopped talking at the meetings; he's not interested in picking a fight. Even though Leslie is lively in general, the meetings have really taken a turn for the worse. You know you need to speak to Leslie about how she's making others feel, but, like Simon, you really don't want to confront her. She's just going to deny anything's wrong anyway, so there's really no point. And even if she doesn't deny what she's doing—since she knows there's some truth to your words—she would hold a grudge for a long time and you don't have the energy to deal with her drama. Weeks go by, and the meetings get progressively worse. A few people ask if they could be excused from attending the meeting, so you know the time has come. You approach Leslie and after spending a few minutes shmoozing, you mention that she's coming across controlling in the meetings. You tell her that it's been going on for a while but you didn't approach her right away as you wanted to see if things would improve. She responds by saying that if it was really an issue, you should have approached her sooner.

Ouch.

When an issue arises, and you notice negative behavior continuing, confront it *right away*. Having an upfront conversation now helps avoid a lot of negativity later.

As an aside, the same would hold true for calling to offer a friend condolences or support during a trying time. Waiting to make the call to avoid discomfort is not just wrong but inconsiderate. And in this case, writing a card to avoid the discomfort of calling is also not ideal.

Here's a good general rule of thumb: *Growth comes from discomfort*. If you're not sure what the right thing to do is in a situation, you're probably trying to avoid the more uncomfortable option. That doesn't mean you need to work harder to accomplish things just to avoid problems. This general rule provides you with a moral compass for what is the right (appropriate) choice in your next stage of growth.

 ## Story

Bert was a non-profit recruiter who was supposed to call to encourage young professionals to attend a variety of events. He didn't love the phone, however, so instead he figured that since the purpose was the touch point, he could send them a variety of greeting cards, emails and texts. But when other recruiters were bringing 25 students to a program, Bert was only bringing six, despite having reached out to hundreds of students.

Texting and emails are great supplements, but they will never replace human touch.

PART II

CHAPTER FIVE

The Art of Setting Goals
Why Documentation Is a Necessity

StickK.com is a goal-setting website. Many of us have goals we want to reach but forget about them as life gets busy. Lose 20 pounds, write a book—trust me, that's a hard one!—volunteer at the food bank. Instead of allowing goals to slip away, visitors to stickK.com enter their goals and make them public by sharing them with the rest of the stickK world. Dean Karlin,[5] a co-founder of stickK.com, found that people were significantly more successful in reaching goals if they signed a contract committing them to achieve their goals. StickK.com enables that process. It is writing down and committing to a goal, and sharing it with others, that makes the difference. Users at stickK.com have a much higher percentage of reaching their goals than others, especially when they are incentivized by monetary goals. (An 87% success rate, in fact.)

When stickK.com was launched, there were many naysayers: Does the honor system really work? Would people actually use the app? Today, with over 600,000 users, it's become a solution for many who find it hard to reach goals otherwise.

According to the stickK.com website "Our mission is to redefine goal-setting using Behavioral Economic principles that empower

---

[5] Dean Karlan is a Professor of Economics and Finance at Kellogg School of Management at Northwestern University and Co-director of the Global Poverty Research Lab.

personal change in any setting. We believe that with the right combination of incentives and accountability, anyone has the power to transform their goals into reality."[6]

But there's another even more crucial, and exceedingly simple, pre-step in reaching a goal: choosing the goal and writing it down. Most people are afraid to choose a goal and hold themselves accountable. Choosing the goal *and* committing to the goal are half the battle. Committing to anything, even a small goal, increases your chance of reaching it. Verbalizing and sharing your goal with others increase those chances even more.

At this point, it makes sense for us to dig into the goal-setting process. It may seem to deviate from the topic of this book, but, in fact, it is crucial in holding employees accountable. Without proper, documented goals, our employees could never be effective. And so we must understand the topic wholistically, in order to get practical at the end. So sit back and come along for the ride.

HOW TO CHOOSE A GOAL

As we delve into the process of goal-setting, the most crucial step is choosing a proper goal. We dance between selling ourselves short and dreaming about unrealistic, fascinating possibilities. In this chapter, we are going to discuss how to choose a goal, when to document proper goals using the art of vision-setting, how to crush those goals, and finally how to inspire others to achieve greatness as well.

---

[6] https://www.stickk.com/aboutus#mission.

The Goal is a Realistic Stretch

Yes, we all know you want to lose 30 pounds by summer, but can we be honest? You either don't have 30 pounds to lose, or you have a bit more than 30 pounds (read: a lot more), and have tried many diet fads without success. Now, that doesn't mean this next attempt can't be the one time where you are successful, but unless you want to be in the hospital for malnutrition, or you've suddenly started training for the ironman competition, you probably won't hit the 30-pound mark.

You know your company's last 360-degree performance review has led you to understand that you aren't providing enough management support for your 10 direct reports. But declaring that starting tomorrow you're going to meet with all reports for 90 minutes a week—up from zero minutes—is a great idea. But it's probably not going to happen for more than a week (if that), especially considering that you have a very demanding schedule and are often on the road. Starting with a goal of meeting with each of them for 30 minutes weekly, or five of them for an hour a week, rotating bimonthly, provides a more realistic roadmap.

Many of us are dreamers. We don't *want* to settle. Small goals aren't exciting. They aren't motivating and surely won't inspire the team to engage. While this logic sounds reasonable, our aim here is not to be cool or flashy. The goal is to hit targets, not just to get yourself and everyone around you hyped. There is nothing wrong with a good kickoff, but that is not what will keep the team motivated.

I'm not saying you should settle for mediocracy. The goal should be a stretch for you. It just shouldn't be such a big stretch that you pull a muscle. Dream, and dream big. Set a long-term vision for yourself. But when you set the goals, make sure they are a realistic stretch. Lose five pounds this month, maybe, or win three new, significant clients this year. Don't go crazy, or you'll end up quitting midway. We all need to see the light at the end of the tunnel, but when the tunnel competes with the great wall of China, you've got yourself a problem.

The Goal is Clear and Measurable

Gallup helps their clients "create exceptional workplaces and engaged customers," with more than 4,000 organizations using their workplace performance platform. Gallup is truly a leader in its space, the Gallup World Poll representing more than 95% of the world's population.[7] Their own research, they claim, has found that when the clarity of what people expect improves significantly, profitability and work quality improve to a meaningful degree as well.

Often managers shy away from being overly explicit. They do not want to be perceived as "mean" or pushy. They think they are being kind, when in fact they are actually hurting their subordinates. According to a *Harvard Business Review* article, "The Art of Setting Expectations as a Project Manager,"[8] written by Amy Shoenthal, the *USA Today* bestselling author of *The Setback Cycle*, it is critical to be clear, deliberate and decisive from

---

[7] https://www.gallup.com/corporate/212381/who-we-are.aspx.

[8] Amy Shoenthal, "The Art of Setting Expectations as a Project Manager," Harvard Business Review Press, 2023. Prod #: HO7UNT-PDF-ENG.

the outset. As she points out, we often fancy terms like "ready for next steps" or "ready for client approval," and they sound great in meetings. But everyone may be sitting there thinking to themselves, "I have no idea what this guy actually wants from me."

Shoenthal continues: "'Leaders tend to have the expectation that everyone thinks the way they do,' says Lindsay Dunphy, founder and project management lead at Firefly Consulting Services. 'So they don't necessarily set the groundwork for employees to work within the systems they've created. Being able to articulate that expectation can be challenging.'" When a new employee arrives at the scene, they are entering only with their previous frame of reference. They know how things were done at their previous job, but they have no idea what's in *your* head. Being more explicit when setting goals doesn't make you meaner. It makes you more clear, and it helps the employees you manage better understand what they need to do to reach those goals.

S-M-A-R-T GOALS

Terms like "increasing sales" and "stopping the bleed" and "employee engagement" sound nice in theory, but they do nothing to help your team progress. You've probably heard of SMART (Specific-Measurable-Attainable-Relevant-Time Bound) goals. SMART is an acronym first written down in 1981 by George T. Doran, a consultant and former Director of Corporate Planning for Washington Water Power Company. It reminds us how to set proper goals. Although the entire acronym is helpful, the most important letter is M for measurable.

Your goal must have two components. It should be specific and tangible, and it must serve as your north star and tell you where to spend your time. It will measure how far you are from hitting your goal ***and*** when you know you have hit it. Let's delve in.

S - SPECIFIC

- Every Goal must have a number attached to it. How many donors will you solicit? How many participants will be in your program. How many children will you service? How many employee check-ins will you have?

- Some goals can have two parts—a minimum goal and a stretch goal. Perhaps you want to hold the team to a minimum standard, but you don't want the bigger achievers to sell themselves short. Or you have a minimum fundraising goal for the viability of the project you are supporting. But you also have a bigger goal, to roll out the program at its optimum level.

- Goals should be documented with start and end dates. And those dates should be as specific as possible. How many times a week will you work on the task and for how long at a time? How many times a week will you exercise and for how long?

Many of us are afraid to spell out our goals because we don't want to be held accountable. But by not stating your goals, you have omitted the very first thing you need to do to reach your goals.

If you do not set a goal, you will not reach it. Otherwise, you are shooting an arrow and then drawing the target around where the arrow lands. It might look like you've hit the bullseye but, in fact, you haven't done very much at all.

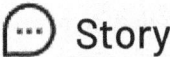 **Story**

Non-profit X was in negotiations with its program director about her salary. She was asking for a raise, based on adding fundraising to her list of tasks. The leadership team asked her for a ballpark figure for how much she thought she could fundraise, and she replied that she would be willing to commit to fundraising between $25K and $50K in her first year. They allowed her to take on the additional responsibility and offered to increase her salary an additional $10K if she raised $25K, and raise it $20K if she raised $50K.

The program director was very upset. She said she did not want her salary to be tied to results and wanted to earn an additional $10K just for taking a stab at fundraising, regardless of whether she was successful. The leadership team eventually acquiesced and gave her the increase based on her future attempts.

While I can't tell you more about the discussions that followed, I can share my feelings about it. In essence, I believe that both parties were mistaken in their approach. The program director was a coward: We all want more money with no metrics attached, but that is not how we grow. We gain skills and develop ourselves by raising the stakes. She lowered the bar and turned the role into a joke.

Yet the leadership team was wrong, too. They shouldn't have allowed her to make a mockery of them. If they needed her in the fundraising role, and she didn't want to tie her salary to her results, then they should have tied her salary to her efforts. They could have returned with any of the following offers: We will give you $10K for "taking a stab" at fundraising provided that each week you do the following:

- Make five fundraising calls
- Write five fundraising emails
- Attend one community event

These action items could easily have been measured and so they could have stipulated that if she does not accomplish them, then her salary would drop accordingly. The key here is to tie her salary to her efforts, *not* her results. I will expand in greater detail below about the OKR accountability and management system, which I first introduced in Chapter One in the section about accountability. For now, what it is crucial to understand is that *the key way to drive results is to hold people accountable for how they spend their time*. But because this takes more time than just checking key performance indicators (KPIs) quarterly, most people opt out. Often, the thing that takes the most time is precisely *THE* thing that we need to do. The choice is up to you: Do you want to do what's right or what's easy?

Your North Star

An added benefit of choosing goals (provided they are goals that you stick to) is that they give you a compass, a north star, if you will, that helps guide your time-management decisions. If you've decided to increase staff retention by 10% this year, you'll prioritize your 1:1 staff meetings and quarterly reviews. If you've committed to cutting expenses, you'll become the DOGE. And if you're motivated to lose weight, you had better be dusting off your sneakers and spending time on meal-planning. Always having the end game in mind is key to staying on track.

Setting the Vision

We've spoken about choosing goals appropriately and how to measure them, but the million-dollar question is knowing which goals to focus on. Should we zoom in on increasing sales or retaining clients? Employee satisfaction or innovating our services? The truth is that in order to know what's next, you really need to know what's first.

Goals vs. Visions

Close your eyes. Think about your business, your program, your venture. Why did you begin it in the first place? What's the dream that lit that fire? Goals are short-term thinking: How much do I want to earn this year? What's our three-year, five-year, or 10-year game plan? But a vision is something bigger. It's not just your why. It's not even your BHAG—your Big Hairy Audacious Goal that

Jim Collins and Jerry Porras discuss in their book *Built to Last*.[9] In fact, it's the opposite of a goal. Your vision is the dream you will *NEVER* see fully realized. It's not the carob tree that bears fruit in 70 years. It's not the business you build for your children's future. It's a dream that is so big that it's impossible to reach. But it's a dream you're willing to spend your life chasing anyway. Because if we shoot for the stars, we just might reach the moon.

Examples of visions that are *not* actually visions:

- I want my company to hit $50M in revenue.
- I want to write 10 books.
- I want to run a marathon.

Examples of true visions:

- I want to eliminate all cancers from the world.
- I want to ensure every child in public school meets their grade level for reading.
- I want to solve the conflict in the Middle East.

Here are some great examples of company vision statements.

- **LinkedIn:** *"Create economic opportunity for every member of the global workforce."*
- **Nike:** *"To bring inspiration and innovation to every athlete in the world"*

---

[9] James C. Collins, Jerry I. Porras, *Built to Last: Successful Habits of Visionary Companies*. HarperBus, 1994. ISBN #: 0887306713.

- **Shopify:** *"To make commerce better for everyone"*

These examples are all bold and virtually impossible dreams—"every member of the global workforce," "every athlete in the world," "for everyone." Daring to dream is what differentiates stronger statements from weaker ones. Remember, the goal for the vision statement is that it is not attainable.

Here are some weaker examples with an explanation for each one.

- **IKEA:** *"To create a better everyday life for the many people"*

Honestly, I don't even know what this is saying. And who are the many people? Let's just move on.

- **Instagram:** *"Capture and share the world's moments"*

Sounds like a great tagline. But you've probably accomplished this already and have nothing else to strive for.

- **Microsoft:** *"To help people throughout the world realize their full potential"*

I really feel like this is off brand. Perhaps Microsoft does want to do this, but this truly doesn't resonate. And again "to help people"? They've probably manifested this vision already by having helped a few people by now.

- **TED:** *"Spread ideas"*

    Again, great for a tagline, not a vision.

- **Tesla:** *"To accelerate the world's transition to sustainable energy"*

    It's nice, it could be bolder.

- **Uber:** *"We ignite opportunity by setting the world in motion."*

    This must have been created using ChatGPT and I have no idea what they're talking about.

Again, a vision statement is not a tagline or a summary of what you do. It is a bold dream that only true visionaries would dream, one that calls for relentless pursuit, an almost maddening obsession and an unapologetic focus.

M - MEASURABLE

There is one key difference between a goal that works and one that doesn't. That is the ability to measure it. It's terrific to "eat healthy" or "go to bed earlier" or "compliment your employees more," but unless a goal post is set up with a specific number attached to it, anything can be viewed as success. If you ate three slices of pizza and fries, but chose water over soda, you have eaten healthier. If you go to bed at 1:15 a.m., instead of 1:30 a.m., you have gone to bed earlier. And if you set an alarm so you remember to compliment an employee more often, and you did it once this month, you have complimented them more. Have you done more? Yes. Have you *really* done anything? Likely, no.

Now you might ask: "What do you mean? I used to eat four slices and go to bed at 3 a.m. and scream at my employees every day. Isn't this an improvement?" Of course, the answer is yes, and I still think you get the point. Of course, gradual improvement is a good thing. But you need to be heading towards a goal. Again, hitting a mark and drawing the target around it afterwards is counter-productive. Remember, we are looking for a stretch in your goal.

Examples of proper goals:

- I want to ~~eat healthy~~ ***drink eight cups of water a day***.

- I want to ~~go to bed earlier~~ ***go to bed by 12 midnight on weekdays***.

- I want to ~~compliment my employees~~ ***start all my employee check-in meetings with positive feedback***.

Your M is not just a goal post. It is also a distance marker. Not only does it tell you which direction to head in, but it also helps you measure your progress towards the goal.

If you start tracking your water intake and realize you're only drinking three cups a day, you understand you have your work cut out for you. On the other hand, if your goal had been to "eat healthy" and you drank three cups of water, you'd feel like a million bucks. It's all a matter of perspective. Measurable goals help you to make and assess real progress.

A – ATTAINABLE

How large a goal should one set? Every year on January 1, millions of people make pledges for a new year with more exciting results. This will be the year they buy their first sports car, or make amends with their estranged family or run their first marathon. Although choosing a big goal is exciting, research shows that realistically attainable goals are more likely to be met. American psychologists Edwin A. Locke and Gary Latham, in their 1990 book *A Theory of Goal Setting and Task Performance*,[10] proposed that specific and challenging achievable goals lead to better performance than vague or easy ones. Again, these goals are relative to the starting point. If you have never run before, a 5K race would be a more attainable goal. If you have already completed a half-marathon, a full marathon might be next. Knowing your initial mile marker is key when trying to gain the most yardage.

But why is it harder to reach a big goal. Is it only because of its size?

According to Philip Gable, professor in the Department of Psychological and Brain Sciences at the University of Delaware,[11] one key reason people fail to reach their goals is that they don't plan out the smaller steps required to get there. We will commit to a very large goal but are unable to strategically plan the smaller steps needed to achieve that goal. What that means is that setting a big

---

[10] Edwin Locke and Gary Latham, *A Theory of Goal Setting and Task Performance*. Pearson College Division, 1990.

[11] https://www.udel.edu/academics/colleges/cas/units/departments/psychological-and-brain-sciences/our-people/philip-gable/.

goal is not the root of the problem. Our problem starts one step before that, in creating a road map for success.

A Road Map for Success

What is executive functioning? According to the Cleveland Clinic, a world-renowned non-profit academic medical center, "executive functioning refers to skills that you use to manage everyday tasks like making plans, solving problems and adapting to new situations."[12] People who have trouble reaching goals due to their lack of ability to plan accordingly, and thus have difficulty creating a road map for success, often have low executive-functioning capabilities. For people in this category, using tools like task-management apps, calendars and setting timers can make a big difference. Additionally, using organizers to break down tasks into smaller steps, as well as adopting more structured, daily routines, can significantly improve planning and organization. I want to emphasize that these aren't just nice suggestions. Breaking down goals into smaller benchmarks is one of the key distinguishers of those who are able to *CRUSH* their goals, compared to those who just watch in disbelief from the sidelines.

---

[12] https://my.clevelandclinic.org/health/articles/executive-function.

R - RELEVANT

When using SMART goals, R for relevant refers to the fact that your goals should align with your values, your long-term aspirations and overall objectives. It ensures that your goals are not just random pursuits but contribute to the end result. But let me share a little secret with you: Do you know why we don't reach our goals? It's because we *randomly* choose tasks that we hope will eventually lead us to our goal.

I have this kind of exchange almost daily:

SMALL BUSINESS OWNER: "I'm having a hard time getting clients."

Me: "What have you tried?"

Owner: "I post on my WhatsApp status, I post on Instagram and I advertise in the local newspaper."

Me: "Interesting." (FYI, Interesting is a buzzword for "I don't even know what to say right now...") "Why did you choose to do those things?"

Owner: "Not sure. A few people suggested those ideas to me. And those people are pretty successful at what they do."

Me: "Nice..."

...And here is where it gets interesting...

Me: "I have another question for you."

Owner: "Yes?"

Me: "How often do you make those efforts?"

Owner: "What do you mean?"

Me: "Well, just as I asked. How often are you posting on your WhatsApp status, on Instagram and advertising in the local paper?"

Owner: "Oh, I don't know. Maybe every few weeks, just to stay relevant."

Me: "Do I have your permission to share an idea with you?" (I wait for approval and then proceed). "Do you know the two reasons people don't reach their goals?"

Owner: "Um, they give up too early?"

Me: "I mean, yes, that is definitely true, but let me add two others: The second one, I believe, is even more important than the first. The number one reason is because they randomly throw darts when choosing what things to try. It's almost as if they believe that calling potential clients and drinking caffeine carry the same weight. And the second reason: Because they don't make those efforts consistently. Yes, choosing the right effort to make is key, and you should really spend time deciding what your efforts should be. But, even more importantly, whatever you choose, you should make those efforts on a consistent basis.

> Consistency in pursuing goals is even more important than the effort itself."

Let's pause the conversation with our small business owner for a moment, and think about effort. You start a diet and plan to exercise more. Taking a walk once a week while you are on the phone with your mother isn't exactly going to do much for your waistline. Even if you weren't shmoozing on the phone, and you were focused on a challenging exercise for 30 minutes, doing it randomly once a week won't allow you to see progress either. It might help, and it could be you would lose a pound a month, but that progress won't motivate you enough to keep you going. Exercising three times a week consistently *would* help you see results. Once a week, not so much.

Now I want to add a disclaimer. What I am *NOT* saying, folks, is that if you are trying to get clients, you should spend your time jogging consistently. That is completely irrelevant and will generally not bring you close to your goal. What I *AM* saying is that if you are trying to get new clients, I wouldn't spend hours agonizing between posting on Facebook and Instagram, or messaging/posting on WhatsApp or LinkedIn or Twitter. Yes, I would get advice. Yes, I would choose carefully. And yes, I would pivot if it wasn't working. But what is more important here is not so much the medium, but your consistency in showing up. Post on your WhatsApp status every day, create a reel for Instagram four times a week and advertise weekly in your local paper. Now let's get back to the conversation.

Me: "Can I add one more thing?"

Owner: "Please!"

Me: "Do you want to know the reason why even people who do make consistent efforts don't reach their goals?"

Owner: "Yes, sure."

Me: "It's because they choose the efforts that are comfortable. If you want to reach your goals, you need to get uncomfortable."

Owner: "Please explain."

Me: "Well, staying comfortable means choosing what is easy. Advertising in your local paper is easy: You design an ad and send it in. But the problem is that most people don't sign up for services from a flyer or an ad. They sign up from conversations and from forged relationships. Can posting on LinkedIn help? You bet! Will it help even more if you post consistently? Even more. But nothing will replace those uncomfortable messages you send and calls you make asking for a meeting. What separates the winners from the losers is getting uncomfortable consistently over an extended period. That's the realistic stretch. Don't make your efforts impossible. Break them down into uncomfortable but doable, bite-sized tasks, tasks that if you consistently do them, will give you success. That, my friend, is the winning formula."

This concept is key and I could spend many more pages discussing it. No matter what you are trying to accomplish in life, if you are comfortable in your efforts, you are probably not growing. It is not comfortable to sit down with an employee and explain to them how they really need to show up. It is not easy to apologize to your brother for the way you acted at the family party. And it is not easy to admit that you made a mistake and guided the team incorrectly. But that discomfort is what makes you a bigger person. That discomfort is what causes growth.

The Formula

$$\text{Realistic Stretch} = \frac{\text{Consistent, slightly uncomfortable efforts}}{\text{Time}}$$

or

$$RS = \frac{CSUE}{T}$$

Once you have clear goals with a realistic stretch, don't just write them down. Take out a thick black sharpie and write your goals out on a huge poster board. Then hang them up for all to see.

HOW OUR EFFORTS ARE MEASURED: OBJECTIVES AND KEY RESULTS (OKRS)

I believe it is finally time for me to introduce you to the full OKR system and how it operates, so that you can easily implement it within your own teams.

OKRs (Objectives and Key Results), are part of a management system used by some of the biggest companies in the world—Walmart, Target, Netflix and Google, to name a few. What differentiates OKRs from other systems lies in the simplicity of the system. While KPIs (Key Performance Indicators) measure and track success, they don't teach you how to *reach* success. KPIs look backwards. OKRs guide you forward. OKRs are simple. They measure individual efforts (as opposed to results), with the hope that if we put in consistent (slightly uncomfortable) efforts over time, we should see success. These efforts are tracked and shared across an entire team and employees are encouraged to help each other. The system is very clear and provides an incredible amount of psychological safety. Before I provide an example, I want to preface this next part by sharing that I use OKRs slightly differently than they are meant to be used, in order to further simplify the process. What I call the KRs—key results or the key efforts that lead to results—others call the O, the objective. I am not doing this to confuse you, because OKRs with this twist should, in fact, facilitate tremendous growth. To read all about OKRs, check out the book *Measure What Matters*.[13] Author John Doerr explains the system in extensive detail.

---

[13] John Doerr, *Measure What Matters: How Google, Bono, and the Gates Foundation Rock the World with OKRs*. Penguin Publishing Group, 2018. ISBN-13: 978-0525536222.

Later, I will also compare the benefits of using OKRs with the Entrepreneur Operating System (EOS).

Let me provide an example.

> Company X is attempting to put on a large, industry-wide conference. The company's written goal for the conference is to make $100,000 in revenue in the first year, via sponsorships and participant fees. Their sales team of 10 is responsible for bringing in $75,000 in sponsorships. Rather than team meetings that are a series of discussions around how much money each employee did or did not solicit, the team will use OKRs to center their conversation around their efforts.

TEAM MEETING 1: Decide the O and KRs

- The O: Solicit $75,000 in sponsorships by the time of the event. (SMART)

- The (slightly uncomfortable) KRs: Each team member should do the following every week:
    1. Call 20 potential leads.
    2. Add 15 names to the lead-calling list.
    3. Post four times on social media about the event.

The team leader needs to then create a conditional formatted sheet or Excel document so that the team's efforts can be easily tracked. For example, if they each need to call 20 people, then when one team member only calls two people, their box automatically turns bright red, If one of them calls 12, it's yellow, and if they can call 20, it turns bright green.

Note: it is not enough to do this orally. Each person's efforts must be documented so they can stare at them and face the reality of what they've done, for good or for bad.

	CALL 20 LEADS	ADD 15 NAMES	POST 4 TIMES
Ryan	2	9	4
Diane	12	15	2

● RED   ● YELLOW   ● GREEN

TEAM MEETINGS 2 THROUGH 10

Over the course of the next nine meetings, the team reviews their efforts. Diane and Ryan both share some strategies that have been working for them, as well as some areas where they can use guidance. These reviews continue each week with participants all learning from each other. At times, small gift cards are given out to incentivize consistent efforts. Every few weeks there is mention of the overall goal: "Great job, we are 1/3 of the way there..." but the overall goal is not the focus.

PUT IT IN WRITING, SIGN A CONTRACT

I've already stated that the goal needs to be written down and be visible. Here, I'll go even further: if your goal has been decided by a group, and you're nervous that some of those members will try to wiggle their way out of their commitments, I encourage you to create a contract and have all the decision-makers sign it. This document should include three components:

1. The stated goal(s)
2. The efforts each person is committing to take
3. The efforts each person is *NOT* committing to take

So often, we say yes to everything and end up accomplishing nothing. You might have a board member who, after a few months, has jumped ship and is on to the next big and flashy idea, or a donor who just decided on the next big program you should run and is asking you to veer off course. It's time to say *NO*. OKRs allow us to cut out the noise and only spend our time on the efforts that truly help.

When There's a Problem

In classic goal-setting models, where results, not effort, are being measured, there's often little room to pinpoint the problem. Goals are not being met and the team hits roadblocks that can drag on for months. There may be underperformers who are responsible, but few want to have those uncomfortable conversations. Let's imagine two problem scenarios with OKRs.

Scenario 1: Ryan is constantly showing reds. He's not making enough calls and is therefore not closing sponsors. Each week he meets with the entire team, as well as individually with his manager. Each week, he spews some halfhearted apology about how next week will be better and gives a half-baked reason as to who he wasn't able to reach this week. Now, this might work for one or two weeks, but by week three his manager asks Ryan directly:

> "Ryan, do you want to be doing this? Do you enjoy making calls and soliciting donors? It seems like these efforts are more than just slightly uncomfortable for you."

At this point, Ryan looks at his shoes a few times and then whispers that he doesn't. He'd rather be more behind the scenes. At this point, the company can decide to transfer him to another team if he's a valuable player, or end this miserable situation for both parties.

Scenario 2: Ryan has straight greens week after week. He's a top caller and is unafraid to speak to anyone. But there's one hiccup. He hasn't closed any sponsors. Great. At least we know the problem. It's not that he's lazy or unmotivated. He just needs sales training.

BENEFITS OF THE OKR SYSTEM

- **It's simple.** One of the key reasons why I recommend OKRs is because of the speed with which they can be implemented, as well as the fact that they allow you to discover and deal with problems in a timely manner. There are many great methods out there, but those that involve constantly sitting in meetings that go on for hours create more problems than they solve. I said that I would discuss EOS, one of those other methods, so here we go.

  EOS, or the Entrepreneurial Operating System, has become all the rage. Teams large and small are jumping on board, buying in to the system's goal-setting concepts, and attempting to solve all their business problems. And although it seems promising, what EOS users gain in procedures, they lose in time. EOS is overly complicated, and, in my opinion, for no good reason. Of course, a business needs vision and execution, but does it also need to track KPIs and rocks, using EOS's V/TO (vision/traction organizer) at their level 10 weekly meeting? What happened to good old-fashioned Google sheets? As with innovation, less is often more. Why don't we just set an objective, decide on the efforts we'll make and measure those? Although complicated looks nice and flashy, it is the cause of tremendous backlog and inefficiency.

- **No more "flavor of the month."** Imagine the scene: Your team has been working extremely hard at the KRs they've set up for the quarter. Everyone on the team understands their role and real progress is being made. The team feels aligned and purposeful and is even being rewarded for positive efforts. Then, one day, during a routine staff meeting, the team's visionary—think CEO, board member or any variety of person who loves to dream but doesn't have the patience to implement—announces that there's been a bit of a pivot and instead of continuing the plan as discussed, we will now be working in search of a new, even more exciting opportunity. This flavor-of-the-month mentality is extremely frustrating for the team and greatly impacts morale. Although the presenter *ALWAYS* thinks his idea is amazing, the team usually is not on board, and many often leave or do half-baked work as a result of the pivot. After all, what is the point of doing your best when you'll probably never finish the project anyway?

OKRs prevent the flavor-of-the-month syndrome. When a visionary steps up to announce his shiny new object, it is the job of the rest of the team to remind him that he agreed that the team will be working on the main objective until the end of the year. And, when necessary, they will pull out the contract that this visionary signed and remind him that although his idea is exciting, it will have to wait until the next objective is chosen. This visionary often ranks high in the company, but the OKR-driven conversation is much more effective in preventing the visionary from using their seniority to get their way.

I myself have witnessed this firsthand. In one particular situation, the objective had been carefully chosen, and the full team aligned, and the person who introduced the shiny new object realized very quickly that it wasn't worthwhile for them to interrupt the incredible progress that was being made. Although it was important for him to push the project forward, as funders were pressing him to do so, ultimately he understood that he couldn't succumb to funder pressure. It just wasn't good for the team.

- **No more "stories about Sara."** A third benefit of OKRs, and my favorite, is that they keep us from using stories as a distraction from addressing why we aren't properly focusing our efforts. Picture the scene: You're reviewing the team's OKR and you notice that Peter only made two of his 10 calls. You ask him about it, and Peter responds by telling you about one of the calls that he made to Sara. He launches into a monologue about the call, how impactful it was, how many leads it generated and how it was the best call he's had in a long time. You are so inspired by Peter's call that you praise him and even tell others about it. You then move on to someone else.

At that moment, you failed the system. Peter was supposed to have made 10 impactful calls and he only made two. He used stories to distract you from the fact that he slacked off and wasn't successful. Had you properly followed the system, you would have caught on to Peter's tactics. You still would have been impressed with his call, and even perhaps asked him to guide others. But then, you would have continued with your line of questioning. You would have asked why he hadn't been able to make the rest of his calls and how else he had chosen to spend his time. You also could have offered to meet over the coming week to help him better clear his schedule so that he can make his 10 calls. After all, if just one call can be this incredible, imagine the impact of nine more! To be clear, it is great that Peter's call was successful. Let's just not become distracted by his stories about Sara, or Marc or Shirley, and let's ensure everyone is prioritizing the efforts that need to be their focus. Work the system properly, and you will see game-changing results.

At this point, you might understand why I title the OKR workshops I lead "How to Get Your Employees to Quit Before You Fire Them." No, I am *not* trying to get everyone fired. And yes, I am sometimes brought in to help with "special situations." The OKR system allows for an incredibly safe environment, and calls for consistent check-ins with employees so that when there is a problem, it doesn't have to drag on for months and years. Gone are the days when problematic employees, the ones who aren't interested in growth, the ones who aren't interested in doing the work, stay on payroll because we don't have the heart to pull the plug. In fact, with OKRs, it is so clear to employees what they need to do, that when they realize they are incapable of doing it, they often leave on their own. In short, I couldn't recommend another goal-setting system more highly.

DIFFERING PERSPECTIVES ON SETTING AND REACHING GOALS

In 2011, Grant Cardone, one of the top sales experts in the world, released his signature book, *The 10X Rule*.[14] In it, he states that true success requires one to set goals that are 10 times higher than what is normally considered necessary. For someone to hit these 10x goals, they need to take massive action and have an entire mindset shift. Playing small is out. To win, you must always play big.

In 2023, Dan Sullivan, creator of the "Strategic Coach" and author of over 30 publications, and organizational psychologist Dr. Benjamin Hardy collaborated to write *10x Is Easier Than 2x*.[15] The book builds on Grant Cardone's theory and states that, in fact, setting a 10x goal can actually be easier than setting a 2x goal. To accomplish a 10x goal you need to work harder, not smarter, and spend your time on activities that will most move the needle, i.e., leveraging what works. In order to accomplish this, you also need a huge mindset shift, as it can be quite scary to aim for such big goals.

---

[14] Grant Cardone, *The 10X Rule: The Only Difference Between Success and Failure*. Wiley, 2011. ISBN-13 978-0470627600.

[15] Dan Sullivan and, Dr. Benjamin Hardy, *10X Is Easier Than 2X: How World-Class Entrepreneurs Achieve More by Doing Less*. Hay House Publishers, 2023. ISBN: 978-9388302852.

THE ART OF SETTING GOALS

In July 2025, *The Science of Scaling*,[16] released by Dr. Benjamin Hardy and Blake Erickson, challenged my thoughts about realistic stretch goals. In the book, the authors propose that rather than setting incremental goals, or even 10x goals, one should set "impossible goals." And accomplish them within an extremely short timeline. Imagine you have a goal to retire with $10 million. Hardy would challenge your thinking:

> "Why $10 million? That's too realistic. What number would feel impossible? How about $100 million?"
>
> "Are you insane?" say I. "You want me to retire with $100 million dollars?"
>
> "No," he answers back, "I'm even crazier. What about if instead of retiring with $100 million dollars, you made $100 million in the next seven years?"
>
> "That really *is* crazy. I'd never be able to do that. First, I need to get X degree, then I'd need to start a company and bring it at least X amount of revenue per year, then...."
>
> "Exactly," he'd say. "You wouldn't be able to do any of those things. You'd have to do something entirely different to reach your new, outrageous goal. You

---

[16] Dr. Benjamin Hardy and Blake Erickson, *The Science of Scaling: Grow Your Business Bigger and Faster Than You Think Possible*. Hay House Publishers, 2025. ISBN #: 9781401967635, 1401967639.

couldn't spend the time studying for a degree. You couldn't wait five years to start a company. You'd have to 'raise your floor' and only say yes to the activities that will get you to that impossible goal."

Hardy's work directly contradicts the work of American management psychologists Edwin A. Locke and Gary Latham, who stated that goals must be achievable. (See earlier in this chapter, where I describe the "A" in SMART.) They felt that if goals are seen as impossible, individuals might reject them and their performance would suffer. I personally have gained from *all* these contradictory concepts, and have used them time and again. And believe me, they work. Not only do I use them, but I talk about the ideas they offer, and I spread them in a lot of my workshops and everyday conversations. At the same time, I still stand behind my belief in the OKR system.

OKR doesn't obligate us to stay small. In fact, I've seen dramatic change and huge growth with the use of the OKR system. My formula still holds true for most of the goals we want to reach:

$$\text{Realistic Stretch} = \frac{\text{Consistent, slightly uncomfortable efforts}}{\text{Time}}$$

The difference is that I am mostly focusing on efforts, rather than constantly reevaluating the goals. Both theories work, and can work at the same time. Each just comes from a different focus point.

There are also a few downsides to choosing an impossible goal:

1. Locke and Latham state, as we saw above, that there is one caveat when choosing goals and that is that they must be achievable, or perceived as such, in order to maintain motivation and effort.

2. To reach an impossible goal you might need to take massive action. That action can be positive, and you might have the full support of your family and friends. But sometimes massive action can come at the expense of family time, of simple pleasures and of your mental health. Before choosing to embark on a goal that feels impossible, take the time to reflect honestly on your emotional and physical state and that of your loved ones. Not every goal is worth pursuing, and sometimes there is a better time to pursue it. If you're not sure, ask your loved ones directly. Their advice is often the best.

Regardless of which theory most appeals to you, and which system you choose for pursuing your goals, remember that goal-setting must be accompanied by *PUTTING YOUR OBJECTIVE IN WRITING!* Don't just state your goal. Write it down. Write it again. Trace it. Etch it in your memory. Hang it on your wall. Put it on your desk. Tell it to the world. Email it out.

Hold yourself accountable. Suffice it to say, it's worth it.

RESOURCE:

SCAN ME

Download a "Documentation & Communication Toolkit", with ready-to-use scripts, confirmation language and documentation templates that support the concepts related to this chapter, at

meiraspivak.com/putitinwriting

CHAPTER SIX

Innovate on Demand

Exactly What Is Worth Writing on the White Board?

Picture the scene. You're sitting in the conference room participating in a brainstorming session. You and 14 others have gathered to solve the latest crisis and you are adequately equipped to predict the outcome. How many more meetings can you sit in where there's a facilitator at the whiteboard asking participants to "think out of the box" and spew innovative solutions? You're encouraged to suggest as many ideas as possible, even if they are out of budget or completely unrealistic. By the end of the session, there are about a hundred impractical ideas on the whiteboard and the only thing you leave with is a headache.

Now the reason you can picture the scene is because you've lived through it dozens, if not hundreds, of times. Every brainstorming session looks the same, with some including variously sized sticky notes with all kinds of scribbles on them—including "innovative gadgets" like silly putty and fidget spinners. I myself have sat through many and have always felt frustrated at the end. In fact, any time I spoke up during the session it was to challenge the idea of suggesting irrelevant ideas, and the response I invariably received was that I was being a Negative Nancy and dampening the mood. I knew that there had to be a better way, but I didn't know what it was.

True story. And it's not a joke. I once sat through a meeting where the facilitator led a serious talk about how the team was in dire straits and needed to make real cutbacks in order to get us back in the game. Time crept by, and you could feel the energy in the room gradually dissipate. An hour into the meeting, the facilitator looked at her watch and realized she still had another 30 minutes. "You know we have another half an hour," she told us. "Let's spend this time thinking big. Let's dream. Let's brainstorm. If the sky were the limit, what dream programs would you run? Don't let money stop you. This is the time to dream." She then went on to facilitate a classic brainstorming session where people shouted out a hundred, out-of-budget ideas that would never be used—and this after the facilitator, at the top of the meeting, had started by announcing to the group that there was no money to spend on extras. I was baffled.

But everything changed for me one day a few years ago, when a coworker handed me the book *Inside the Box: A Proven System of Creativity for Breakthrough Results* by Jacob Goldenberg and Drew Boyd.[17] Hmm, creativity is a skill, not a gift? Anyone can innovate on demand and turn challenges into opportunities if they just follow templates, even if they were not born creative? Brainstorming sessions that last two hours, not two days? I was hooked, but immediately faced a problem: The book delves into what's called the Systematic Inventive Thinking (SIT) innovation method,[18] and clearly spells out, for example, how to innovate toilets and refrigerators on demand. Huh. I was more involved

---

[17] Drew Boyd and Jacob Goldenberg, *Inside The Box: A Proven System for Creativity for Breakthrough Results*. Simon & Schuster, 2014. ISBN #: 978-1451659290.

[18] https:www.sitsite.com/about-us-systematic-inventive-thinking/.

with sales and relationship-building. Could those two areas be innovated on demand as well? So, I did what most people *don't* do: I reached out to one of the authors, Jacob Goldenberg, who was the cofounder of the SIT method. I asked him for a meeting to better understand the theory. He offered to set up a zoom call, and eventually went on to train me directly for several years to become a facilitator of SIT. Additionally, over time, I was trained by Drew Boyd, as well.

SIT innovation is taught in the biggest business schools in the world, including Wharton, the London School of Economics, Harvard and Stamford, to name just a few. Numerous articles have been written about SIT, and yet even now surprisingly few people have heard of the method. About 80% of the world's inventions were created using SIT, although the inventors created them without realizing it, and when using the method would have saved them significant time and resources had they known about it. One of my missions is to get SIT out into the world, as it has changed the way I face challenges, and I know it can help others.

Before learning SIT, I would freeze when faced with a problem. My instinct was to say that if things weren't working out, then, well, "everything that happens is for the best," as I was trained to think that way growing up. And although I still agree with that statement, it didn't guide me in my next steps. I still spent a lot of time sulking and feeling negative. Now, years later, with SIT in my back pocket, I am equipped with exact, step-by-step instructions for turning challenges onto opportunities. It has truly allowed me to pivot more quickly, and to get excited when a conflict arises. Because I truly know that the best is yet to come.

To fully teach all of SIT is beyond the scope of this book, although I do run a variety of workshops for teams who want to learn how to become a leader in the innovation space. Giving these workshops is tremendously energizing, as SIT—and teaching it—has impacted so much in my life. Before we get to the subject of what needs to be documented and written on the whiteboard, let's start with some background about SIT and its key concepts. Understanding them will help frame up the most effective way to brainstorm.

WHAT IS SIT?

Systematic Inventive Thinking is a brainstorming method that follows templates. To many of you this might sound bizarre. After all, in the past when you have tried to innovative, you might have thought to find a calming setting—a lake nearby, perhaps—so you'd be in the right state of mind for generating innovative solutions. SIT claims that this is unnecessary, that you can brainstorm from any office desk anywhere at any time, regardless of how relaxed or tense you feel. Just as every song and every detective novel follows a template, and creativity typically soars in those spaces, so, too, following templates is key in innovating. What SIT breaks is fixedness, a cognitive bias that limits us to seeing an object or structure only in the way it's been traditionally seen or used. In doing so, it allows us to think on an entirely different plane.

THE FIVE TEMPLATES

Here is a brief overview of SIT's five templates.

1. **Subtraction.** Often when we try to innovate solutions, our gut tells us that we should add services, add programs, add features. But with innovation, less is often more. Imagine this fictional scene: You're eavesdropping on a past Apple board meeting. As you listen in, you hear that they are trying to innovate the iPod. (Remember the device that gave us music at our fingertips?) Someone suddenly offers a suggestion: What if we subtract the touch screen? What?!? You almost gasp out loud, forgetting that you're eavesdropping. And he continues: While we're on the topic, let's subtract the iPod's control dial, too. This way, no one can choose the exact song they want. Instead, the songs will come on randomly. By now, you've heard it all. Is this guy crazy? Apple had invented a device just for people to carry around songs *AND* choose the songs they want to hear. And now someone is suggesting that those two exact, incredible and unique features be eliminated? Are they off their rockers? Well, maybe they were. And perhaps the 450 million people who used iPod Shuffle were, as well! Subtracting key features from the iPod allowed Apple to sell to niche markets, such as runners. And represented a tremendous improvement. So, the next time you want to innovate, try subtracting.

   Author's note: As someone with an extensive background working with non-profits, I want to issue a warning that subtraction is hardest for non-profits. When organizations are emotionally tied to services they offer, when subtracting a program means impacting "Sara's experience," it feels almost wrong. But growth is not always comfortable, and sometimes subtracting an offering is a necessary step. Try to think beyond the here-and-now when you make these decisions, and focus instead on the overall health of your organization.

2. **Division.** Division is the innovation template that we use when innovating a process or procedure. Currently, the way we typically do things is the way we've always done them. Why fix what's not broken? But often that "fixed" nature is the root of problems. Think about your onboarding process. Currently, when you hire a new employee, on their first day they sit through a number of meetings, overwhelmed by the information they're asked to absorb. They take pages of notes, and try to comprehend as much as possible. Now imagine if the process is divided, and onboarding doesn't start on day one. Perhaps it starts two weeks before, on the day the new employee was hired. What material was sent to the employee before they started, and were they paid for reading it? What welcome gift were they sent? Imagine how much more prepared they would feel when they finally walked through the door on day one. It used to be that when we went to a store to shop, we were expected to pay for our purchases on the spot. The invention of credit cards has divided the process. Today, we can buy now and pay later. Similarly, by dividing the airline check-in process, airlines

enable us to check in much earlier than if we have to do so at the airport. Using division can truly revolutionize the way we approach conferences, meetings and myriad other processes.

3. **Task Unification.** How often have you said, "We've lost another employee. How are we supposed to manage when we are short so many staff. Losing one was manageable, but some of these people were key." You've tried reaching out to recruiters, you've tried posting on Indeed. To no avail. Well, you are in luck. Task Unification is the SIT template that we can use when we are short on resources, whether it be staff, money or time. We ask ourselves the following question: Who among our current resources can help us solve our problem? Instead of looking outside, we look inside and see who or what can partially or fully help us lift some of the burden. Instead of finding a new CFO, for instance, perhaps the job can be taken by someone else at the company. Please note that in order for this question to be helpful, you must be committed to breaking fixedness and to changing your old ways. You will be challenged to see resources in different ways than those you're accustomed to. Rising to this challenge will change the way you brainstorm. Later we will be discussing Task Unification in the context of using writing to help us brainstorm.

4. **Multiplication.** If you've ever tried to create a new product line or a variation on one, but aren't sure what to do next, multiplication is the SIT template for you. When using

multiplication, we copy the product we already have and then change it in a counterintuitive way. The first razor had one blade. Just adding a second wouldn't be innovative. That's addition. With multiplication, we will change something about the second blade—its position, its edging. The market today now sells shaving razors with as many as seven different blades. The change is what makes it creative.

5. **Attribute Dependency (AD).** This is by far the hardest template to learn and is the basis for the SIT app Omnivati.[19] We use this SIT template to look at products and determine where to create or break dependencies. Attribute Dependency is often used to create smart products. Think smart glasses, where the color of the lens *DEPENDS* on the strength of the sun, or smart windshield wipers, where the speed of the wipers *DEPENDS* on the strength of the rain pouring down. When MBA students learn SIT, they are challenged to innovate the NBA, just as the Savannah Bananas team is starting to do for baseball. (The Bananas play a version of baseball with 11 unique rules, including a two-hour time limit, no bunting, allowing batters to steal first base and fans to catch foul balls for outs.) Currently, in a standard NBA game, the number of points you receive *DEPENDS* on how far away you are from the basket when

---

[19] A "cloud-based platform that offers a toolkit for rapid and systematic generation and management of ideas," Omnivati was founded in 2019 Jacob Goldenberg and Rom Schrift. https://www.omnivati.com.

you took the shot. Perhaps it should *DEPEND* instead on whether or not the shot touched nothing but net, or was a hook shot. Currently, ticket prices *DEPEND* on the team's current standing. Perhaps they should depend on how well the team scored the week before. AD allows us to consider disrupting the status quo and consider many alternatives.

THE CLOSED WORLD

The title of Goldenberg and Boyd's book introducing SIT includes the phrase "inside the box"—rather than outside the box—to suggest that the way we classically brainstorm is somehow flawed. Think about it: When you've sat in brainstorming sessions and been told to "think out of the box," has that helped you generate creative ideas? Was the suggestion helpful that if you somehow just thought harder, you would come to a better conclusion? If you are like almost every person in the world, I'd assume not. When instructed to innovate, your brain doesn't know where to go to be able to do that.

Let me invite you to enter the Closed World, an imaginary space where we find our solutions within. We do need to tell our brain where to search. So, we give it parameters: Only search within the pool of people who work at this office, or only search for solutions that cost less than $10,000. By creating our closed world, we narrow down options, forcing our brains to innovate. Instead of telling it to think of anything, we tell it to think of something very specific. That guides our thinking towards potential ideas. Think about this idea: When you work on a puzzle, what is the first step? The borders, of course. A jumble of puzzle pieces on the table is overwhelming, but when there's a structure to follow, your brain feels more settled. What is most counterintuitive about this is that the more restrictive the closed world, the more innovative the solution will be! We think that in telling someone to think out of the box—the sky's the limit, we tell them—we are helping him to innovate. The truth is that he will end up frustrated and inhibited. And not very innovative.

CHANGING THE CLOSED WORLD

The Closed World instructs our brains where to look for solutions. But what happens when we still feel stuck? Sometimes, the answer is to change our closed world by zooming in and out. Just as a camera zoom gives us a different perspective, so will zooming in and out of the challenge. Imagine you are trying to innovate your hotel check-in process. What do most hotels do? They put chocolate chip cookies at the counter. Wow...how innovative. (Detect the dryness of my words.) But imagine you zoomed out a bit and asked when the check-in process actually *could* start. Perhaps it could start on the shuttle van on the way from the airport. Perhaps, as I board the van, when I'm handed a cup of coffee and told to enjoy my short ride. Now imagine that you zoomed out further and suggested that the check-in process could begin when I book my hotel online. As soon as I book, I might receive a call: "Hi, Meira, we are so excited you'll be staying with us. What is your favorite newspaper? We'd love to have it ready for you when you arrive in the hotel." Wow, now that's impressive.

Think about the onboarding process at your organization. When does it start? When the new hire arrives at the office? What would happen if their experience with you began the moment they are hired? What information, videos or gifts are sent to them beforehand? Imagine if they were paid for any work they do for you prior to their hire date. And what about your conferences? When do they actually start and end? Currently, conferences start from the moment participants check in and end when they leave. Often, as soon as they walk out the door, they forget most of the knowledge they acquired. Perhaps pre- and post-conference programs would make a world of difference.

GETTING DIABETES MEDICINE TO CHINA

Drew Boyd shared the following example with me in one of our training sessions together. Imagine that you work for a pharmaceutical company, and you want to introduce into the Chinese market a drug to cure diabetes. China is a huge country, with more 1.4 billion people as of 2024. The thought of trying to achieve that kind of reach is pretty daunting. How can you possibly get your drug from the US to diabetics in China? Sure, if you look at the challenge from this perspective, it is definitely overwhelming.

The key is to change our perspective. Instead of imagining the drug reaching everyone in the entire country, zoom in and see if you can get it to one city in China. Now zoom in further and see if you can get it to a town in China. How about to one neighborhood? How about to one home in that neighborhood. In that home lives a 65-year-old man. Can you get the drug to him?

Here's the thing. If you can't get the drug to one 65-year-old man in China, there is no way you will get it to the entire country.

But if you can get it to him, you can scale the model to get it to others. At that point, you zoom out and see if you can get it to other neighborhoods, towns and cities. Eventually you're thinking about reaching everyone in China.

Keep changing your perspective and you'll discover incredible opportunity.

WHAT MAKES AN IDEA CREATIVE?

For an idea to be creative it should have three components. It should be original, useful and simple. Original makes sense, of course. The idea wouldn't be creative if you plagiarized it. Useful we can understand as well. If coming up with a million random ideas for addressing a challenge yield nothing useful, the exercise has been useless. The last component, simple, is, I believe, the key, the component wherein SIT's impressiveness lies. When you use the SIT templates, you generate solutions. Some of them are completely out there, but the best solutions are mostly the ones that leave you feeling "Oh, that's so simple, why didn't I think of that?" It is solutions that are close to you, that are so simple, that make a world of difference.

Here's an example that may be helpful. If you have raised or cared for children, then you know how hard it is to take their temperature when they are sick. They squirm, doing everything in their power to not stay still. And unless you have a second person helping you who can hold down the baby's hands and feet, you often just admit defeat. Enter the pacifier thermometer, a pacifier that also takes a baby's temperature. The idea is simple. Babies like pacifiers. Use the Task Unification template and give the pacifier another job. So simple. Yet so effective.

WHAT ARE THE BENEFITS OF A CHALLENGE?

Whenever I run SIT workshops, I stress how important this question is. In fact, I believe it is one of the most important aspects of brainstorming and opening up to new ideas. Let me take a step back and explain another core principle of SIT: Function follows form.

The idea is simple. Instead of seeing challenges as challenges, SIT sees them as solutions for something, although at the time, no one is sure what that something is. If a chair broke and the legs fell off, instead of designating it as garbage, SIT will ask the following question: What are the benefits of a chair with no legs? Who would want a chair with no legs? What can we use it for? And after some thought, possible solutions might include a beach chair, a gaming chair, a booster seat and a porch swing. Instead of seeing the problem, choose to see the solution. And when doing so, always list a minimum of three to four solutions, as the first and second you think of are often pretty weak.

I know that challenges *are* real. I am certainly expecting that you will not jump for joy if your CFO suddenly quits. But knowing you have five SIT templates to apply to that problem is exciting. When SIT is done correctly, the new solution might even be an improvement over yesterday's.

💬 Story

During Covid, and before the world hired remotely, I had a challenge. One of my staff, who had been part of the team for eight years, decided to move. He was a recruiter of sorts, and most of the work entailed running programs, building relationships and recruiting for further programs. And now I was stuck. As the world shut down, someone suggested I hire remotely. "Are you kidding me?" I asked. "You want me to take an in-person, relationship-building position and just fill it with someone remote? It will never work!" But then I stopped myself, as SIT has trained me to understand that every challenge is an opportunity. So I paused, and I asked myself the million-dollar question: What are the benefits of hiring someone to work remotely? At first, I froze up and continued to list all the downsides. And again I stopped myself. I committed to listing three to four potential benefits. "Well, it would definitely save money, since we wouldn't be running in-person events. And I guess that person wouldn't spend so much time driving, shopping and planning, and they would have more time to spend in one-on-one meetings. And well, I guess they could be hyper-focused on those meetings and as a result develop even more relationships…" Well, by the time I finished my list, I was definitely open to the idea. Let me share with you two things that resulted from that change:

1. Not only did the plan work, the person I hired was so talented and so focused that he ended up recruiting more attendees than we had ever hoped for.

2. The next year, I went back to hiring in-person.

The second is an extremely important point. You must be open to *all* solutions, even if they are not ideal or they don't entirely fix the problem. As long as the solution is good *for now*, it can prove to be very positive. Don't worry about solving all of life's problems. For the moment, just alleviate the problem facing you now.

EVERY CHALLENGE IS AN OPPORTUNITY

You have a choice. When challenges come your way, you can choose how to approach them—as challenges or as opportunities. I don't say this lightly, but how can it be that two different people could go through the same medical crisis, and one person came out depressed, bitter and estranged from their family, while the other actually feels more connected to their family, friends and religion? Since there is no difference in what they experienced medically, it comes down to a matter of choice. Just as stress is a choice, so, too, is your approach to challenges. Remember, your approach won't actually change the situation, but it will definitely change what happens next.

PUT IT IN WRITING

When you run a brainstorming session, writing ideas down is key. In this case, I am definitely *not* referring to the notion that writing down a million ideas on the whiteboard is productive. I think by now you know that that's not how I approach brainstorming. Here, I am specifically referring to listening to the resources you have around you, so that you can hear and utilize the ideas that surface that could be solutions.

Earlier, I introduced the third SIT template, Task Unification (TU). It's the template that we use when we are short on resources. We use TU to utilize the resources we currently have to solve our problems. But here's the thing. Most of us aren't even aware of the resources we have around us. We just don't think about all the people and things in our lives. When we need to find a job, we might think of our immediate friends and family, but do we think about previous coworkers, community leaders and past workshop attendees? The TU template allows us to do just that.

Let me first define some SIT terms. **Components** are what we have to work with, what we can utilize as needed. There are two types of components: **internal and external**. The internal components are what's inside a component, what's a part of it. External components are what is around, and relevant to, a component. For example, I have a cup of coffee sitting on a table. The internal components of the cup consist of the coffee inside the cup, the sides and base of the cup and the handle of the cup. The external components are the table that the coffee cup sits on, the lady drinking the coffee and the cookies on the table. Notice I didn't say the garage or the lady's guitar. Those factors, although possibly nearby, are not relevant to this situation.

Here is an example to illustrate the idea of components.

> Bob is struggling with the work-life balance—or imbalance—in his life. His parents are aging and need extra assistance, and he still has a wife and kids at home who need him as well. He is an only child, so all the responsibility is falling on him. He is starting to feel overwhelmed, and that's taking a toll on his mental health. Bob isn't really sure where to turn.

APPLYING THE SIT PROCESS

When using any SIT template, as we are about to do for Bob's situation, the first step is always to define the closed world, the place where your brain is allowed to go to look for solutions. In this case, Bob analyzed his finances and decided that he can't afford to hire care for his parents. He still needs to put his kids through college and his parents didn't save much money for care. He also decided that he can't have his parents move in with them, they just don't have the space. His parents need about two hours a day of care and he needs to figure out what to do.

After defining the closed world, the next step is to list all the components that we have to work with. When using TU, we list both the internal and external components. Here, writing down the components is key, and without doing so, you will certainly miss solutions. Note that your internal component list will probably be longer than your external one.

Bob begins to list his internal and external components:

INTERNAL:

- Wife
- Kids – Laura, Charlie
- Aunts/Uncles/Cousins – Joanne, Jill, Greg, Mitch, Lauren and Leslie
- Neighbors – Jones, Swartz, Hill
- Doctors/Nurses – Dr. Jon, Nurse Angel, Nurse Dave
- Coworkers – Steve, Allison, Aron
- Clergy – Pastor John
- Golfing Buddies – Neil, Scot and Howard
- High school friends still connected – Laura, Mike, Don
- Members on the board he serves on – Riley, Tom, Victoria

EXTERNAL:

- His parents' neighbors – Smith, McKenzy, Jordan
- His parents' friends – Clinton, Depaul, Lucas
- Organizations his parents previously volunteered at – Youth Core, Scouts of America, Big Brother/Big Sister
- Organizations his parents donate to – St. Vincent Hospital, Red Cross, St. Mary's High School

After finishing his list, the next thing Bob needed to do was to randomly select components to see if any of them can help him solve his problem. After selecting it, and before saying "that's a useless idea," take a moment to think about using that component to help you solve your problem. Ask yourself: What are the benefits/should we use it? If it's a possible or terrific idea, write it down and save it for later.

Bob randomly chooses his neighbors. He wonders if they would be interested in helping with a once-a-month shift. After all, he has helped them out a bit. (Bob also used the Division template to simplify the process by allowing multiple people to help for shorter slots). He definitely liked the idea and wrote it on the possibility list. He then selects "organizations his parents donate to," and realized that perhaps he can ask St. Mary's if they can start a rotation of high school kids who might be willing to visit his parents to earn community service hours. Bob realized he struck gold with this one as he was familiar with St. Mary's program. He was so ecstatic that he decided to stop to make calls and finish the SIT exercise later.

The important piece to note here is that the odds are pretty slim that Bob would have come to the idea without listing his resources as he did. The discipline of writing down the list is the key exercise here. Don't fall into the trap of doing this quickly. Don't just write "coworkers." List them out. And when you're stuck, zoom in and out. Think of very specific people and then let your brain think more generally. When you are stuck, keep changing your closed world and you should have no problem generating solutions.

Imagine you are the owner of a supermarket and you are trying to figure out a way to get your customers to stay in the store longer when they come in to shop. Your closed world is that you don't want to spend money or hire anyone new to reach your goal, and you only want to use your current resources. You list your components:

INTERNAL:

- Produce
- Food
- Deli
- Carts
- Cash Registers
- Employees
- Shelves
- Aisles
- Starbucks
- Bakery
- Floral Dept
- Coupons
- AC/Heating
- Music, A/V
- Lights
- Shelves
- Floors
- Pharmacy

Please notice that if this were a real example, you wouldn't just list your "employees." You would break the list down further—cashiers, stockers, cleaners.

EXTERNAL:

- Customers
- Signage
- Parking Lot
- Nearby Stores
- Lights
- Cart corrals

You then randomly select one of the components and imagine using it to keep customers in the store for a longer time each time they visit.

Carts, for instance. If I slowed them down a lot, people would certainly stay longer in the store...

Now, I know what you're thinking. That's ridiculous. People would be so upset if their carts barely moved, they wouldn't stay in your store for even one minute. They'd leave in disgust. And yes, you wouldn't be wrong. They would be upset. But that is not the point of this exercise. Not every idea will be a good idea, but going through the SIT process will get you thinking differently. The next time you or someone on your team wants to shoot an initial idea down, stop them and go through the process. Don't stop after one bad idea, the rest might be pure gold! Let's Imagine that the carts didn't drive slowly but actually had a charging station, so people could charge their phones while they shop. Hmm. That would definitely keep some people in the store for longer. I know if my phone was dying and I didn't have a way to charge it, and a store offered a free charging service, I definitely would end up roaming and spending money as I waited for some charge. Hmm, an idea that seemed terrible is now a real option.

Let's try another example.

> How can you use Starbucks to keep customers in the store? Well, the barista can definitely prepare the drinks at a slower pace. That doesn't sound too exciting. Well, let me share how a Vistage[20] group member responded after participating in an SIT workshop. He, too, had selected Starbucks and wondered about the possibility that the entire store check-out went through Starbucks. That would definitely slow everything down. Then we thought further: What if Starbucks was sold at check-out? If I was waiting to check out, and someone was right there selling and preparing Starbucks, I would be enticed. Ordering and waiting further would keep me in the store for longer. While I was waiting, I might grab some snacks on the shelves.

Think about it. If this was a classic brainstorming workshop and a moderator in the front of the room was asking participants to think out of the box and figure out how to keep customers in the store for longer, they might have listed some ideas—give out

---

[20] Vistage is an executive-coaching organization for small and midsize businesses. http://www.vistage.com.

free samples or more coupons. But would they have suggested moving the cashier to Starbucks or sell Starbucks at the cashier? Probably not. Listing out components that seem irrelevant, even insignificant, is what makes the biggest difference.

One final example.

> You are the owner of a high-end interior-design firm and have just lost your chief of staff. You only work with three clients at a time, as each one receives your undivided attention and represents multimillion dollar projects. You went through four of the five stages of grief over your chief of staff's departure—denial, anger, bargaining and depression, but never quite reached acceptance—and have eaten about five tubs of ice cream. Now you feel even worse, of course, and decide to try the normal avenues for filling job openings. You've hired recruiters, listed descriptions on Indeed and Craigslist and posted on LinkedIn. Nada. Zilch. Zero. You're at the end of your wits.
>
> You know you've exhausted all channels and are ready for SIT, so you set out to define your closed world. Now you are no longer looking outside. You need to find a solution, even a temporary one, from within your current resources. So you make the list.

INTERNAL:

Your team:

- COO
- CFO
- CMO
- Principal Designer
- 5 Designers
- 15 Junior Designers
- HR Director
- 2 Bookkeepers
- 3 Project managers
- 4 Procurement managers
- 1 Executive Assistant

EXTERNAL:

- Current Clients – The Milton Project, The Pink Building, The Community Room
- Past Clients
- Five Board members with expertise in finance, HR, legal, marketing and design
- Competition – PDC, Opal Design, New Wave

YOU THINK ABOUT THE CHIEF OF STAFF POSITION AND THE KEY ROLES:

- Project management
- Performance tracking

- Facilitating communication across teams
- Strategic planning

Applying the Division template, you ask yourself which of your resources could take care of any of these jobs.

You begin with project management. Who can help with this? Wait a minute, you already have three project managers on staff! Didn't Marsha just approach you about wanting more responsibility? I mean, she won't be perfect but promoting her will ensure more longevity here. Furthermore, what about if *all* project managers knew that after being here for two years, they would be eligible for a promotion. That would make their job more enticing from the get-go, a valuable commodity. You realize you're on to something. What you see here in these few sentences is one of the strengths of SIT at play, and that is that it always asks you to consider the benefits of an idea.

As for performance tracking, your CFO might be able to do some of it, but in case they need more help, can your board member with an expertise in finance help? Perhaps they work pro bono in the beginning, but if you see it takes longer, could they receive a consulting fee? The CFO can also have the project managers pull consistent reports so he can analyze data on a more consistent basis. That's not perfect, but definitely okay for now.

And perhaps, for right now, you take on the other roles. Stop, I know what you're thinking. Me? You want me to take on *more*? I am already so overwhelmed. I hear you. But answer this question: What are the benefits if you facilitate communication and oversee strategic planning? Well, it might actually simplify things. Until now, I was having three meetings a week to ensure that the chief of staff knew what to do. I can actually spend that time doing the work. It would only take me one hour and I'd save two more. Hmm. And I would save a lot of money. The chief of staff was paid $350,000. Honestly, saving the meeting time is enough for me.

These examples show you how putting ideas in writing is an integral part of making SIT templates work. Like all the other templates, Attribute Dependency (AD), also involves a lot of writing in its innovation structure. With AD, we not only discuss components (what we have to work with) but also discuss attributes (adjectives that describe the components). The AD component is complicated, and only works well if it is used properly. In order to help your team use AD properly, you might like them to have access to the Omnivati app. If that is the case, please be in touch. It is an invaluable tool. For now, I will offer an extremely simple matrix just to help you understand how AD works. Of course, it is imperative that you fill in the matrix and do not just do this verbally. It will otherwise be impossible to use it.

Imagine you own an IT company and want to rethink your client contracts so as to make more money. Currently, you have 10 clients and you charge them based on the number of hours an employee works on a client's account. If you pay your employee $50 an hour, you charge the client $100. If you pay your employee $100, the client pay $150, and so on.

In order to use the AD template, you first write down your company's internal and external components:

INTERNAL COMPONENTS:

- Employees
- Software
- Office
- Contract
- Billing

EXTERNAL COMPONENTS:

- Current clients
- Past clients
- Vendors

Note that in an actual scenario, you would list each client specifically.

Because you would like to innovate the way you make money, you now spend time WRITING DOWN the attributes of your billing system:

INTERNAL ATTRIBUTES:

- Time frame of billing
- Pay-back dates of billing
- Pricing of billing
- Payment options for billing

EXTERNAL ATTRIBUTES:

- Speed with which clients pay their bill

Next, you create a matrix with both the internal and external components down the left of the matrix and the internal components *only* across the top. Mark the boxes that are on the diagonal or above the diagonal with an "X" to prevent repeats.

	BILLING TIME FRAME	BILLING PAY-BACK DATES	PRICING OF THE BILLING	BILLING PAYMENT OPTIONS
Time frame of billing	X	X	X	X
Billing pay-back dates		X	X	X
Pricing of the billing			X	X
Billing payment options				X
Speed of clients paying billing				

Next, begin by choosing a box and ask yourself if a dependency already exists between that box and any other box in the grid. If it does, then ask yourself if the dependency is beneficial and should remain, or should be broken. If there is no dependency, ask yourself if there should be.

	BILLING TIME FRAME	BILLING PAY-BACK DATES	PRICING OF THE BILLING	BILLING PAYMENT OPTIONS
Time frame of billing	X	X	X	X
Billing pay-back dates		X	X	X
Pricing of the billing	Pricing depends on billing time frame		X	X
Billing payment options			Payment options depend on pricing	X
Speed of clients paying billing				

Idea 1: There is a dependency between the pay-back dates of the billing and the time frame of the billing: Currently, the client pays $100 an hour regardless of how many months you billed for. What if you charged them more if they were being billed for a longer period of time? That means, for instance, that you might bill them at the end of each month that they paid $100 an hour, but that if they only billed at the end of each quarter, they were billed $120 an hour?

Idea 2: Currently, the rate they pay depends on who does the work. What if the rate they pay depends on the form of payment they use? If they pay with a check, they pay $100 an hour, but if with a credit card, they would pay $110.

In this way, using AD gives you a new way to approach problem-solving. Again, SIT might not provide the perfect solution to your problem. But it will give you new ways of thinking every time. But remember: Write it down.

CHAPTER SEVEN

Holding Effective Meetings

We've all been through them. It's as if our bodies instinctively know to yawn as we enter the room. We've heard about enough paradigm shifts and big ideas to last our lifetime, and no one needs to be told yet again to think out of the box. So how do we upgrade our meetings? How do we ensure that they are not only productive but also effective?

A key element in effective meetings, one that I have discussed in passing earlier, is psychological safety. The concept was explored in the 1950s, and was later popularized by Amy Edmondson, a Harvard Business School professor.[21] The concept is as follows: In order for people and teams to thrive, individuals need to feel safe speaking up about both the positive and the negative. They should feel comfortable sharing an idea that's been percolating inside them, and comfortable sharing opposition to someone else's suggestion. Psychological safety does *NOT* mean that an entry-level employee has a vote in decisions made at the highest level of an organization, but it does mean that she should feel safe speaking up when asked for her opinion. In order for this kind of comfort to exist in an organization, staff in higher-level positions need to create a psychologically safe environment, one in which their staff can thrive and be successful.

---

[21] Amy Edmondson, *Psychological Safety* (HBR Emotional Intelligence Series). Harvard Business Review Press, 2024. ISBN: 978-1647829964.

Edmondson's study examined the extensive effects of psychological safety. It found, not surprisingly, that those experiencing greater psychological safety were more satisfied with their work schedule, the relationship they had with their supervisor and their opportunities for growth and development. Safety in the workplace leads to more productivity; its absence is extremely detrimental.

CREATING SAFE MEETINGS

Meetings are an especially effective time to establish and maintain psychologically safe environments. Picture this scene: Ten executives are sitting around a big conference table ready to begin the meeting. Abruptly, the big boss walks in, muttering under his breath. He's clearly unhappy with how his day's been going and he lets everyone around him know it. He starts the meeting by asking the company's vice president for an update on the recent merger. Clearly not sure how honest to be, the VP hems and haws, nervous about losing his job if he makes the boss even more upset. The boss bangs on the table and demands that someone take the blame for the recent typo in one of the company's advertisements. When no one owns up, he becomes further enraged, and announces that he's freezing everyone's salaries until someone explains to him what's going on. He gets up and leaves and doesn't forget to slam the door on the way out.

Although this scenario isn't real, many of us can actually relate to some of the elements of the story. Perhaps, we've been in a room where the "boss" has a temper and makes everyone nervous about getting things wrong. This could be an adult "real boss" or the bully in a classroom. Perhaps the "boss" made sure we knew that only one answer would be tolerated. Were we threatened with being fired, or kicked out of the group, if he isn't satisfied with the status quo? Or maybe he creates an even more hostile environment by shouting, blaming and slamming doors? If any of these situations resonate with you, you have been in a situation with limited psychological safety.

So how do we prevent meetings like these from happening? How do we create spaces where people feel safe to speak up about both their successes and their failures? How do we allow team members to take ownership of their work, without worrying about their own job security? And of course, how can we create meetings so effective that employees want to participate in them, and aren't looking at their watches the entire time? In short, we are trying to accomplish two things: leading effective meetings and preventing fear-ridden ones.

A BLUEPRINT FOR LEADING EFFECTIVE MEETINGS

Step 1 – Setting Expectations

When people are invited to attend a meeting, two key questions pop into their heads.

- What is the purpose of the meeting?
- How long will the meeting last?

If you can't answer those two questions (and, some might joke, provide snacks), you are not entitled to hold a meeting. Instead, take some time to reflect on the answers to those two questions, and only then schedule your meeting.

The Real Purpose of the Meeting

Yes, a meeting agenda is helpful. And yes, a meeting agenda with set times can keep everyone on track. But when I say "the purpose," what I mean is: What are you *really* trying to accomplish? Dig deep. Do you really care about the meeting or do you want people in the room simply to listen to your voice? Do you have a message to share, or do you just want to establish authority? Are you having this meeting because you need your colleagues' input? Spend some time writing down the purpose. Seeing things in writing in front of you allows you to process more clearly.

Often when guiding others to decide whether to share a certain topic, the following questions can help determine if you are creating safe emotional spaces. Why are you sharing this information—for their sake or for your own? If you are sharing it because you think it will be helpful for them, great. If it is because it is exciting or fun for you, you need to decide if sharing it is appropriate in that situation. It might be completely appropriate to speak to your spouse about a challenge you are having with a child. It might not be appropriate to share that information in a public forum, just to get it off your chest. Before you call the meeting, ask yourself what its *real* purpose is. Once that is clear, share the reason with those being invited. Nobody wants to be left guessing as to whether or not they are about to waste their time.

And nobody wants to show up at a meeting that has an agenda they don't feel prepared for.

Here are some good reasons to run meetings:

- To inform your team of a new project and to divide up tasks
- To increase team morale/comradeship
- To get team input on a new idea
- To get feedback on _____
- To hold the team accountable (positively, as well negatively)

Here are some reasons *not* to run meetings:

- So, you can say you ran a meeting
- Because it is already on the calendar
- To review information everyone already knows (Send an email instead, if it's really necessary.)
- To get a picture of you running a meeting
- You get my drift...

If expectations are the key to disappointment, then *managing* those expectations is key. Let people know if this meeting isn't covering any new ground, for example; It's just for teambuilding. Let them know to come prepared with updates on a project. And let them know that updates are coming (whether good or not). Emailing this information beforehand allows people time to process and mentally prepare for the ensuing conversation. The same applies to meeting length. Let them know how much of their time you need.

Here is a great sample message that can go out before your teams' offsite.

Dear Team,

I am excited about next week's offsite. I wanted just to send a short note so you can be best prepared for it. The point of the offsite is for the team to spend time together before we head into budget season. Although there will be four sessions over the two days, most of our time will be spent learning more about each other's personalities, our likes and dislikes and best ways of working together. I hope that when we finish the meeting, we will all have a better sense of how we can optimize our work together. The meeting will last from 9 a.m. to 5 p.m. both days, with a formal dinner on night one. The company will be providing all meals and travel, and sending you home on day two with a to-go dinner for the plane. Looking forward to greeting you at XX address on Monday between 8:45 and 9 a.m.

Thanks,
Sincerely X

How Long Will the Meeting Last?

I happen to be someone obsessed with time. When I forget my watch, I find myself glancing at my bare wrist 10 to 20 times an hour. I aim to show up to meetings either on time or early. And my biggest pet peeve is...can you guess? Yes, wasting time. I don't want to waste your time, and I don't want you to waste mine. If we have a meeting, please don't cancel right before—I could have done something else with that time. If we have a meeting, please help make the conversations engaging and allow for meaningful participation.

But even if you aren't as time-obsessed as I am, I assume you value your time. After all, it's our most finite resource. When planning a meeting, let people know the start and end times, and be mindful of those times. Write the timing down in advance, in the email, and on the agenda. When a meeting does need to go over time, announce that you know time is up and that if anyone needs to leave, they should feel comfortable doing so. If key people need to leave early, it's better to schedule a follow-up meeting, so that no one feels they might be missing out on key discussions.

Meeting Follow-Ups

In line with the title of this book, it is imperative that every meeting follow-up is in writing. That can include the meeting recap, next steps, project deadlines and next meeting times. This can be done via email, but WhatsApp or internal apps can be utilized as well. Having things documented in black and white eliminates plausible deniability. According to Wikipedia, "plausible deniability is the ability of people...to deny knowledge or responsibility for their actions..." By sending a follow-up email in writing and asking for confirmation, you remind everyone of their responsibilities. When team members know their roles, they feel safe and are ready to hold themselves accountable.

Step 2 – Gathering Feedback

Meetings are a great way to gather feedback about how well a program or product is performing. Perhaps the new pension structure isn't as well received as you anticipated. Maybe your employees aren't appreciating the work "culture," not enjoying the need to hustle till 10 p.m. on weeknights and answer phone calls on the weekends. Or maybe employees are unhappy about how you've doubled down on OKRs and asked them to make more phone calls. The question isn't whether or not they are happy. The question is whether you are creating a space that is safe enough for them to speak up about it. Remember, the answer isn't always yes. But everyone deserves an answer.

So, how do you create a space safe enough for them to speak up—not only in a situation where you think they *should* feel comfortable, but where they actually *do* feel comfortable? I want to preface my answer to these questions by saying that you probably won't create a space where *every* single person will feel comfortable. And that is okay. 100% is not the goal. Someone might have extreme social anxiety that you won't be able to fix. Someone else might be in the middle of a fight with a coworker and doesn't want to share in front of them. And a third person might be stewing from an earlier zoom and is completely distracted. The goal is for you to know that you did your best to ensure the safest outcome.

Step 3 – Allowing for Anonymous Responses

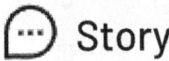 ## Story

I had a virtual role in helping a non-profit improve their "sales," i.e. their recruitment of participants in their signature program. As part of the training, the team was asked to call potential participants and to record some of those conversations. During the team meetings, those recordings would be played and everyone would be invited to offer words of praise and suggestions for upgrades. We found that the same people would always speak up. The others? Crickets. Then one day I received an email from one of the crickets, the non-speakers, asking that they not be called on during the meetings. A few days later, I received a similar email from a second silent participant. Because I try to have direct conversation with people, rather than trying to avoid being uncomfortable, I brought the challenge up at the meeting: How can the group learn and improve if some of us are afraid to offer and receive feedback? In response, we spoke a lot about cultivating a growth mindset. Nevertheless, I needed to put a better plan in place.

I was familiar with the Slido.com app,[22] and had used it for other purposes, but now I realized it would be the perfect solution for this problem. Slido promotes itself as "the easiest way to make your meetings interactive." And although that is probably true, I would rephrase it as "the easiest way to make your meetings psychologically safe." The app enables meeting hosts to engage with participants through "live polls, Q & A, quizzes and word clouds," essentially providing you with different tools for making meetings more interactive. But an engaged crowd doesn't necessarily mean a safe crowd. Yet Slido, whether realizing it or not, has somehow done both.

How I've Used Slido in the Past

Slido has a feature called live Q and A, which allows participants to suggest questions anonymously. Additionally, once those questions show up on the leaderboard, other participants can anonymously vote on whether they like the question, giving the question a virtual thumbs up or down. Doing so improves the question's ranking, ensuring that it's more or less likely to be asked. This enables more controversial questions—and questions normally swept under the rug—to gain visibility. Imagine this scene: An MC and three panelists sit on a stage near a large screen. The MC invites the audience to anonymously submit questions via the app, and they are

---

[22] https://www.slido.com.

then displayed on the big screen. As participants start to like or dislike questions, the ranking for each question can change. Panelists are watching the action live, shifting uncomfortably in their seats, praying that they don't have to answer certain questions. Their fate is determined by the preferences of the audience, and a very lively and engaged panel ensues.

How I Use Slido Now

Although I would still use Slido for a panel today, the main way I use it has shifted. Let's go back to the MC and his three panelists to explain what I mean. Many in the audience were still hesitant about feedback. They felt too badly about giving negative feedback. And although that sentiment was coming from a good place, the team couldn't grow without it. If your work is never critiqued, how can it improve? Here's where another feature of Slido is very helpful. This feature allows presenters to create an open text box. The presenter can use it to ask a question and participants can post answers anonymously. Everyone can see the responses but can't give feedback. They can only start a new line and submit their feedback.

Downside of Using Slido in This Way

Because feedback is completely anonymous, people often feel free to be more harsh in their critique. It is much easier to write "I think your voice sounded too nervous and unsure of yourself," than say it in public. Made publicly, such a statement probably would have been sandwiched between "Wow, I love how you got straight to the point" and "You ended really strong." Additionally, waiting for people to keep typing is slower than stopping and then typing again, especially when multiple people are participating. It definitely takes more time.

And the Story Continues…

The team was still complaining that they didn't feel it was nice to be negative. Again, I'm not saying that we should go around critiquing people. I'm saying that we need to go through this exercise to improve. And here was my verdict: We would still play recordings for the group but there would be two options for feedback. The first, the more ideal way, would be to give verbal feedback. Getting uncomfortable, and having a lively conversation, is truly the ideal. At the same time, we would all access Slido, and people could choose to give written feedback as well. Although not everyone was thrilled with my decision, I was at peace. Again, I wasn't going for 100% satisfaction from every person in the room. But I truly believe I created a space of 100% psychological safety, and that was the game.

When You Meet in Person

Another great way to allow people to provide feedback anonymously is through an old-fashioned lottery. Let me explain.

💬 Story

A team was motivated to provide a high level of psychology safety, and wanted to get "real" feedback from the organization's departments. The team put together an off-site get-together for about 150 people. After providing a delicious meal, the excitement began. I started by asking the entire group a pre-determined question similar to the following: What can our leadership team do to improve the current environment in our organization?

By now you know that asking a question like that, in front of the leadership team no less, would not exactly be conducive to creating the safest of environments. So, although the question was spoken out loud, it was followed by the following instructions: Please write your answers on the provided index card, *without* your name, and put it into the basket that's going around the room. I will then pick out answers at random and read them out loud. Then together we'll look for patterns in the responses, and see what areas need the most fixing.

Well, that did cause a ruckus, and I really can't commend the leadership team enough for allowing that incredibly safe space to be created. It was clear by the end of the program which areas were most problematic. And the energy in the room was palpable, as employees appreciated the opportunity to share, and trusted that next steps would be taken.

The next time you are running a meeting, or even just gathering information, think about the way you are collecting the data. Can people share freely? Is an anonymous survey that asks very specific questions about the roles and responsibilities actually anonymous? Taking time before the meeting to think about creating a safe space will make a world of difference.

Step 4 – Making yourself approachable

As a leader, you need to create a psychologically safe space, not just during meetings but *ALWAYS*. Your aura needs to be an open one. By that I don't mean that you always have to be available. But others should feel comfortable approaching you about a variety of challenges, because you've shown them that you won't use their honesty against them later. They also know that even if you're upset, you won't blow up in their face or play the passive-aggressive game. Of course, this is easier said than done. When someone comes over to you to tell you that they think you didn't handle a situation well, or that they would have approached a challenge more appropriately, what you want to do is tell them off. But if you want to create a psychologically safe environment, you can't. You can't yell, retaliate by rehashing something they had done in the past that you thought was improper, nor can you reprimand them—telling them that it wasn't their place to give feedback. *EVEN IF YOU ARE RIGHT.* Please understand that this has nothing to do with right and wrong but everything to do with being approachable. This is extremely hard to do, but the payoff is immense.

Now, I know your next question. How is it okay for people to just give feedback, whenever they want, to those at a much higher level in the organization? The answer is that it isn't. It is not always appropriate for younger and/or less experienced people to criticize someone older and/or more experienced. It is not always okay for a new employee to give feedback to a seasoned one. And when that kind of thing happens, we need to tell them that it isn't okay. But *not* at the moment when the less experienced or younger person is being inappropriate. Yes, if they speak in a disrespectful way, they should be redirected to speak appropriately. But when they are critiquing the way the office has been running for the last 20 years, at that moment just thank them for their feedback and tell them you want to think about it, and will get back to them at a later time. And make sure to do that. And then, at a completely separate time, you are welcome to initiate a conversation about how you appreciate getting and giving feedback and allowing them to share their preferences as well. This way, you have made them feel comfortable sharing *and* you have set up better guidelines for the future.

I really want to stress how difficult this is. It means putting your ego aside, time and again, for the greater communal good. It means feeling embarrassed, even in public, but not shaming the other person back. It means holding back on eye-rolling (which is personally very hard for me) and saving it for later. This is ongoing work that will need to be done just about every day of your life. And the feedback you get from the people you interact with will make it all worthwhile.

PREVENTING FEAR-RIDDEN MEETINGS

By now, you understand the work you need to do. Applying the principles to team meetings should be easy. Create a safe space to gather feedback. When the feedback comes, accept it with a smile, whether or not you agree with it. Never yell. Never bang your fists. Never make people afraid to share updates with you. And never threaten people's jobs if they don't give you the responses you want to hear. Might they need to be terminated for a lack of productivity? Yes, but it should never be done publicly during team meetings. Don't forget—you are not just doing this for them. You are doing this for you and for the success of your team. A team that feels safer will work harder, perform better and yield better results.

CHECKING FOR UNDERSTANDING

Another way to ensure meetings run smoothly and people feel safe, is to check, to make sure that your expectations were clear. You can do that by having people verbally summarize the information back for you, or, again, using an app like Slido to gather a written review. With virtual meetings, another way to gather feedback is to have participants type their responses in the chatbox, but only submit their responses on the count of three. This way, everyone submits simultaneously without being swayed by the opinions of others. In any case, the last thing you need is to have a week go by when employees wasted dozens of hours focusing on the wrong thing.

OFFERING HELP

People perform better when they feel supported. I don't need to quote any of the thousands of articles that have been written on the topic. Just know that when you are dividing up jobs, or asking for projects to get done, asking "How can I make you feel supported?" goes a long way. Will you do their job for them? No. But can you keep the door open so they know that if they have questions they can turn to you? Yes. And if they use you as a crutch and come to you too often with questions they should know how to answer, you can give that feedback then. But the meeting is not the moment. Focus, instead, on providing them the feeling of total support.

INNOVATING YOUR MEETINGS

Sometimes, meetings feel stale. Monday morning meetings can be dreadful when the same thing happens each week: Lisa reads the minutes, Brad updates the group on the budget and Charles gives out the week's tasks. Try using SIT to innovate the meetings. By using the Division template, for example, we can rearrange the order of what is discussed in the meeting. Utilizing Subtraction, we could eliminate certain components of the meeting, and using Attribute Dependency, the agenda for the weekly meeting might *DEPEND* on last week's performances, or future projections and timing.

Despite all of the resources that SIT offers, sometimes we just feel stuck and need an innovation reboot. Here, too, is the time to change your closed world. Why innovate your entire meeting?

Perhaps just work on fixing the first five minutes. What can you Subtract/Multiply/Divide from those first five minutes to give you a fresh perspective? Just write down all the typical components of the first five minutes and apply a SIT template. Then try it again with the last five minutes of the meeting, or apply it to the budget update. You'll be surprised by the results.

Epilogue

Writing this book has been profoundly meaningful. When I first started working on it, I told myself that I would just take it slowly and see where it goes. I'd try to write 10 minutes a day with no pressure. Well, after about three or four months with only 5,000 words to show for it, I knew I couldn't continue at that pace. If I did, by the time I finished the book, the examples would be obsolete, and I'd need to start again.

Next, I decided I was going to write 1,000 words a day and finish in over a month or two. That was working, albeit slowly, and I was okay trudging along at that pace.

But then, after listening to Hardy and Erichson's *Science of Scaling*, I decided I would try for an impossible goal—that I'd write 2000 words a day, finishing within two weeks. I was pretty nervous but figured YOLO—you only live once. And I realized that the worst-case scenario was that I might fail to finish. In fact, not only did I hit my goal, I completed the first draft a day early. It still needed editing, but I was very happy with my progress.

I hope that this book has inspired you to CRUSH your own goals, to think differently and to avoid countless unnecessary disputes. If you have gotten to this point in the book and would like to delve deeper into any of the above topics, or have me run a high-impact workshop for your team, please reach out to me via my website, **www.meiraspivak.com**, or contact me on LinkedIn.

Until next time,
Meira

Acknowledgements

I want to thank the many people who have helped me on the journey to create and publish this book.

Thank you to Martha Gellens for doing an incredible job editing this book and patiently working through a lot of my stream-of-consciousness thinking. Any errors are my own! A special thank-you to my brother-in-law, Marc Spivak, for helping with the editing and my incredible husband, Chanan Spivak, for designing the cover. Thank you to Elisheva Lesser who spent hours executing the design, marketing and sales strategy for the book and website, as well as helping to design the book's cover.

I want to acknowledge the outstanding staff at NCSY (www.ncsy.org) and the OU (www.ou.org), who have encouraged my personal development and my work on this project. A specific thank-you to Rabbi Micah Greenland and Daniel Gordon for supporting it, and to Dovid Bashevkin for my first writing course years ago.

Thank you to Jacob Goldenberg and Drew Boyd, who have helped me on my SIT innovation journey. Learning Systematic Inventive Thinking has truly changed my life in many ways, and I am thrilled to give the content over to others.

Thank you to the Vistage community (www.vistage.com) for forcing me to learn my innovation content cold and for being so appreciative of all the innovation workshops.

Thank you to Olami, Charlie Harary and Ben Rapaport, who started me on my journey using OKRs. Learning and implanting them have truly transformed the way I support and manage employees and clients.

Thank you to Jacob Rupp, who helped me begin my business-consulting journey and taught me how to monetize a passion project.

Thank you to Rachel Eden, who has been an incredible partner in crime in the work we do together and who has made me a better consultant.

Thank you to Tiago Pereira for his incredible work on the cover design and interior formatting, and for his attention to detail throughout.

And my thanks to you, the reader, for purchasing this book and believing in me. I couldn't have done it without you.

Made in the USA
Coppell, TX
28 February 2026

72961153R00115